THE PRIMROSE WOOD

To Alexander and Amelia,
Alex, Clementine and Justin
with my love

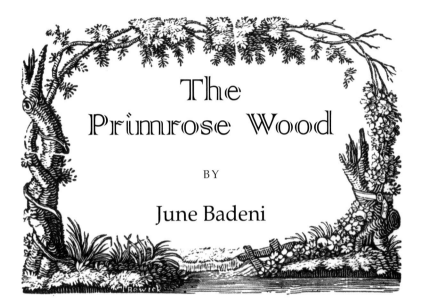

The Primrose Wood

BY

June Badeni

EAST KNOYLE
THE HOBNOB PRESS

First published in the United Kingdom in 2006 by

The Hobnob Press,
PO Box 1838, East Knoyle, Salisbury SP3 6FA

British Library Cataloguing in Publication Data
A catalogue record for this book is available from the British Library.

ISBN10 0-946418-52-7
ISBN13 (from January 2007) 978-0-946418-52-7

Typeset in 11/15 pt Zapf Calligraphic, and Colonna
Typesetting and origination by John Chandler
Printed in Great Britain by Salisbury Printing Company Ltd, Salisbury

CONTENTS

The Primrose Wood   1
The Chestnut's Magic   5
The Autumn Planting   9
The Willow Tree   13
Sticks for the Fire   17
The Pleasures of Stonewalling   21
The Poplars are Felled   25
September Song   29
The Obituary of a Pen   33
A River for all Seasons   37
Shopping in a Kerry Village   41
Unbidden at an Irish Wedding   45
A Shell from the Galician Shore   49
Souvenir from Rhodes   53
Water under the Bridge   57
Hail and Farewell   61

The Mole Trapper   65
The Kingdom by the Sea   69
The Magic Spade   73
Elegy for a Woodcock   76
The Sound of Birds   80
Birds Seen and Unseen   84
In Search of Nightingales   88
Bird-Watching by the Way   92
Disappointing Country   96
Harry and the Captain   99
Living for the Moment   103
The Poachers   106
Spoilt Statesmen   110
His Greatest Pride   113
Drop o' Ginger Wine   117
Roy and Ada   120
Bidda   124
Nanny   131
The Herdsman   134
Muthu   138

ACKNOWLEDGEMENTS

The author and publisher are grateful to Country Life, *in which many of these essays first appeared, for permission to reprint them; also to* Convivium, *in which 'Bidda' was published.*

THE PRIMROSE WOOD

'THE SPRING comes slowly up this way,' Coleridge said, and there is a sweet familiarity which never quite stifles surprise in watching the successive manifestations of its coming. Snowdrop, crocus, celandine; the swelling of the sticky buds on the chestnut trees, like blobs of shiny brown toffee; the monotonous two syllable call of the great tit, the rich, melodious whistle of the blackbird; dust in the lanes, catkins in the hedges. There is, too, the sudden inexplicably joyous capering of a nine-year-old girl, flinging arms and legs about in the warm sunshine – a response to the stirring of the sap, for children who are, in a double sense, closer to the earth than we, *feel* the spring in the same way as birds and animals. Later will come the cuckoo and the lush, green grass and all the prodigality of Nature in its season, but first will come what is perhaps the best of all spring's gifts – the primrose.

Deep in the woods of England, shaded by oak and ash and thorn, the primroses will bloom as they have done from time immemorial, their simplicity a silent rebuke to the vulgarity of the more colourful and sophisticated flowers, their sweet, earthy scent a perfection never to be attained by the costly liquids inside the delicate bottles in the shop windows of London and Paris.

Generations of children have sought them, and picking primroses is one of childhood's dearest memories. It was a ritual – unless the date fell too early – to pick them on Good Friday so that they could be used to decorate the church for Easter. Potted meat jars concealed by a thick matting of rich green moss was their setting, and they adorned the window-sills in profusion.

The wood was close by the little hamlet that gathered round the church and so far removed from the outside world that no one else ever came there; no car-loads of people from the towns ever sought our flowers. A basket and a ball of wool were the equipment with which one set out, and the gate into the wood was the entrance to a special paradise. A hurdle maker worked there. He had a rough shack to protect him from the weather, and because of the donkey and cart that he used to carry his lengths of wood and to convey himself to and from his work he was known as Donkey Jim.

One passed quickly over the parts of the wood where he had been cutting and clearing, for although it was there that the earliest primroses were to be found they were always small and very short in the stalk. It was in the uncleared woodland, in the undergrowth and among the brambles, that the best ones grew – carpets of them in a wild profusion, pale stars lighting up the darkness of the shaded places. John Clare described the flower in loving detail:

> With its little brimming eye
> And its yellow rims so pale
> And its crimp and curdled leaf –
> Who can pass its beauties by
> Without a look of love . . .

There was no need for restraint in picking, for a whole basket could be filled without leaving any trace of bareness on the ground. It was a point of pride to get the longest stalks possible and so one plunged an exploratory finger downwards until it met the root. It was always deliciously damp at the base of the stem and one's finger-nail would often be muddied with worm-casts thrown up by the subterranean creatures who were stirring as the earth grew warmer. Often, too, there would be a dry, dead leaf sticking to the stem, sometimes impaled by it – a meeting of the year that was dead with that now waking to life.

Perhaps it is just a part of the magic that attaches to all the landscapes of childhood – the 'meadow, grove and stream' that Wordsworth found 'apparelled in celestial light'

– but the spring days in that wood had some special quality as though the pale, luminous faces of the primroses were seen in a dream. All around us were white wood anemones in flower and the bright green leaves of the bluebells that would bloom in a few weeks. Like a dream, too, remembered at daybreak, the sounds come back to me; the screech of a jay, the hollow clang as the wooden hasp of the gate shut behind us, the clatter of pigeons rising from the trees, the tap of Donkey Jim's adze.

Our favourite part of the wood was the site of a Roman villa, opened and coverd in again about 100 years ago. There was excitement in the possibility of finding a Roman coin, but the youthful mind, still unaware of the swift flight of time, was not inclined to meditate upon the growth of primroses and briars over the hearth that had warmed men who have now been dust for more than a thousand years.

Today, the wheel has come full circle and more. The M4 motorway has taken the wood in its stride, removing half of it in the process. Man has once again harnessed these acres to his uses, and where the primroses and bluebells grew the biggest service station in England has been established in the name of progress.

THE CHESTNUT'S MAGIC

VERY YEAR, in the early spring, I cut a twig of horse-chestnut and put it in water in the house to watch the brown, sticky bud opening. The pleasure of it comes partly from the beauty of the thing itself, partly from its significance; for no one could fail to be excited and stirred by seeing spring, symbolised by this twig, unfolding day by day and hour by hour before one's eyes. Unfolding, too, a little ahead of time, for one can look out of the window at the buds that are still on the chestnut tree, swinging in the wind against a blue March sky, and know that next week they will be at the very stage that the indoor bud grew out of yesterday.

Beauty, significance – and a third quality is added to them, so that when a visitor, observing the single twig in a jug on my dressing-table, asks if I am reduced to that for floral decoration, I can smile in a rather superior way and say nothing. The third is magic; for it is, if one may be forgiven the simile, like watching a superbly done conjuring trick. Out of a small pocket, the conjuror produces 34 handkerchiefs where there seemed to be only one, and nobody understands how they got there or how they were contained in that small space. Out of a little brown bud, perhaps an inch long and half an inch wide, come a stem, four or five fan-shaped groups of wide green leaves and a blossom made up of hundreds of small flowers. 'Do it again,' the children beg the conjuror; and he does it again, year by year, but the familiarity can never make the miracle less startling. The unfolding of life through seed and bud and flower can never be less than miraculous.

This year I cut the bud, as usual, from the tree outside my window, and brought it in during the snowy weather in February, but this time I decided to keep a record of its growth, with notes and sketches and carefully recorded dates. It was very small, and during the first two or three weeks, when it showed no sign of progress, I wondered if I had cut it too early. But it looked healthy enough. The bud was as dark and sticky as toffee, the stalk pale and smooth, the exquisite little horse-shoes clearly stamped upon it, each showing seven spots like nails round the rim.

On Sunday, March 13, I noted in my log: 'Green tip showing through the brown for first time,' I carried it about following the sun from window to window round the house, and the green tip grew. Five days later, it was showing half an inch. On the 19th I noted that an inner layer was pushing through from under the first piece of green, and on the 21st the green, shiny casing burst, just as the brown one had done, and the leaves emerged though still tightly folded. At this stage I photographed it; it looked like the head of a snake with extended tongue. Then I went away for two days, leaving it in the south-facing window of a warm room. When I came back, all sorts of things had happened. The bud had shot upwards to a new angle, as though the snake reared its head to strike. The brown casing and the green were both left behind, open-mouthed around the vigorous stem. The outside of the bud – being the back of the leaves – could now be seen to be covered with tiny white hairs like the down on a baby's head.

A few days of sun followed, marred by cold winds which did not touch the chestnut twig, secure behind its glass. It grew rapidly. The bud divided into three, each still furled, and the two on the outside presented concave surfaces to the middle, where the central bud had been clasped between them. Each of these furled buds consisted of seven narrow strips, lying parallel like fingers outstretched and pressed together, the middle one longest. As the fingers lengthened and slowly parted, one saw that they were leaves. Seven leaves to match the seven nails in the horseshoes on the stem. John Clare noticed how often the number five occurs in nature:

> For in the cowslip-pips this very day
> Five spots appear, which Time wears not away.

The flowers of bindweed and of bryony, the eggs of many birds, he said, all obey the number five. No doubt one could likewise trace the mystic seven – number of joys, sorrows, sins and virtues – through the natural world, beginning with the chestnut.

The seven fingers of leaf have opened now. Their vivid green is so fresh and brilliant after the long months of dead grass and brown leaves and naked boughs that it surprises one at every glance. All the young, tender, piercing beauty of spring is expressed by this twig. 'I have a longing for life,' said Ivan in *The Brothers Karamazov*, 'and I go on living in spite of logic. Though I may not believe in the order of the universe, yet I love the sticky little leaves as they open in the spring.'

Outside, the north-east wind and the night-frosts keep the chestnut buds hooded against the cold. But as I look up at the tangled branches I know what is hidden in all those brown, sticky blobs. I know that they hold the dancing candle-flowers, as the eggs in the nest in the yew-hedge hold the singing blackbird. And after they have looked like snakes with heads raised to strike, I know that the green shiny casing will split to let through the leaves and the conjuring trick will begin all over again.

THE AUTUMN PLANTING

I HAD BEEN WAITING what seemed an unconscionable time for a dry day, a day not only dry overhead but also sufficiently dry underfoot for the ground not to turn into a mud-pie as soon as one put a trowel into it. At last it had arrived. It was a golden, autumn morning with the dew lying thick on the grass and just a faint smell in the air of the frost which had come and gone while we were still in our beds. I took my trowel and the box full of little bags of bulbs, all neatly labelled, and went out into the garden.

My boots made a track in the dew as I crossed the lawn and another track of larger footprints proclaimed that the master of the house had already passed this way. I could hear the rhythmic thump of his axe from the edge of the orchard where he was cutting a tree. I stood still and listened for the other sounds behind it: the stream at the bottom of the hill was full after the heavy rains of September and I could hear its tranquil, constant voice; the drowsy hum of a tractor on a distant field, like a lazy bumble bee, and the sweet, melancholy song of a robin who sat on the top of the weeping beech. Under its shade not so many weeks ago a 10-year-old boy had pitched his tent – a new and treasured possession – and had made feasts of sardines and potato crisps for all the family in a mess-tin surviving from the first World War. Now he was at his desk far away, doing Latin or mathematics, and the robin was singing summer's end.

I set down my box and surveyed the ground. Here was the perfect place. Already I could see in my mind's eye the brilliant colours of the crocuses, purple, golden, white and striped, the blue grape hyacinths, and the chionodoxas with the name which I love – Glory of the Snow. I began to work. Lift a divot of turf with the trowel, tuck the bulb into place, put back the turf, pat it down. Purple crocus, one, two, three, four . . . Now some golden ones, one, two, three . . . The golden are my favourite. They are the same colour as the bill of the blackbird who will be singing, when they are in flower, his first ecstatic notes of spring.

> *Wonderous, impudently sweet,*
> *Half of him passion, half conceit.*

~ 10 ~

So Francis Ledwidge wrote, sitting in a dugout in France and remembering with the sharp anguish of the exile the peace of his native village in Ireland.

I finished one bag and stood up to ease my back and look round me. The brilliant golden light bathed the old porch which was to be the background for my bulbs. The stone seemed to soak it up, to take some of its colour. It is curious how our Cotswold stone changes in different seasons – sharp and almost white in spring sunlight, silvery grey under snow, golden in autumn. Today it reflected not only the colour but the mood of the day, its mellow tranquillity. Such is the spirit of autumn. April is exciting, disturbing, full of 'divine discontent', whispering not only to youth of lands not yet explored, of all life's vast and boundless possibilities. But October rides upon an even keel, calm, contented; it is the response after harvest, the dying down of the year.

While easing my back and indulging my day-dreams, I wandered over to the orchard to see how the tree-felling was proceeding. I watched for a time while the axe rose and fell and the white chips of wood flew. But presently the sight of so much industry reproached me and I returned to my work. Now for the striped crocuses. Lift the divot of turf, tuck in the bulb, one, two, three . . . And I fell to thinking, despite the forward leap of my imagination, how utterly improbable the whole thing was. When I paused to look at those little dry, brown bulbs that lay in the palm of my hand, it required an act of faith to believe that from them would come the brightly coloured crocuses in whose throats the first emerging bees would linger to take the nectar.

These elm trees where the rooks are cawing with their autumn voices, where the leaves will hang for a few weeks yet, like bright, new-minted pennies: will the tracery of twig and branch soon be seen once more against the winter sky, and will the buds open again to the fresh green of spring? How curious it is, this passage of time, this cycle of the seasons.

The robin sang to me again as I dropped the last 'Glory of the Snow' into its hole and covered it with the turf for its long winter sleep.

THE WILLOW TREE

THE WILLOW was old and hollow, and the shell which was all that remained of its trunk was twisted. Some years had passed since it was pollarded, and the waving branches, catching the fierce autumn wind, tugged too hard at the frail trunk and brought it down. It was one of a row, all old, that stands along the banks of the stream, and two had gone already. From the orchard wall you can watch the sun going down on a summer evening and see its slanting rays touch the cool leaves of these willow trees, and watch their shadows stretch across the grass; and part of the pleasure is that it is a *line* of trees, following the stream. I can't explain why; it has some connection with the fascination of an avenue disappearing into the distance, and with the way my heart turns over at, 'White in the moon the long road lies, That leads me from my love.' But I want that line not to be broken and I want to be sure that it will always be there, between the orchard wall and the setting sun.

So I took some cuttings from the willow trees and grew them, and later moved them out into the field to replace the casualties. The protection I put round them was not strong enough; the horses nibbled the tops, and they died back, sprouted crookedly from the bottom of the stems and were spoiled. But there are more young willows grown from my cuttings, and this time I shall encase them with tree guards. And I shall want one more because of the newly fallen tree.

It had to be cut up. Since willow trees, like all things mortal, must die at last, and since my cuttings will, I hope, grow up to take their place, it seemed a pity to be sad about it, so I took an axe and a saw and went down to the stream on a sunny afternoon and set to work. But I did feel sad for a while. I remembered that the first wren's nest I ever found was in a fissure of the bark of this tree; so neat, it was, that I passed it a dozen times before I noticed. And the nest that a pigeon had built this summer lay crookedly among the branches, almost on the ground; there were some feathers in it, and some old droppings. I thought of the white eggs and the hideous little naked, fleshy bodies, and the still, patient form of the brooding bird, and the throaty, sweet call – coo, *coo*, coo, coo, coo. But the problems of demolition soon occupied my mind.

I like the feel of tools that fit the hand well, and I like the rhythm of axe and saw, and I don't mind knowing that I use them badly so long as I am alone. It is amusing to try to do it better, and after an hour or two one improves and works with less effort. I started with the axe, and at first I listened to the rooks in the elm trees near-by and the dog splashing in and out of the stream; but soon there was nothing else in the world but the ring of the axe and the smooth skin of the willow branches and the deepening white wound. The chips that flew away from under the blade had a clean, sweet, faintly resinous smell and the purity of snowflakes. There was triumph in that moment when, with a creaking sigh, each branch gave way.

I dragged them out, lopped off the side-shoots, beheaded them, separated the twigs and small stuff from the long, clean, smooth poles. Then, with the saw, I attacked a stouter branch. The song of a saw is rather like that of a boiling kettle, only less sibilant, and it has a rhythm of one, two, one, two, instead of a continuous purr. It is a pleasant noise, and while I worked I fell to thinking vague and scarcely connected thoughts about willow trees: the Queen in *Hamlet* telling of Ophelia's death:

> *There is a willow grows aslant a brook,*
> *That shows his hoar leaves in the glassy stream;*

and Lorenzo, talking to his Jessica on a moonlit night:

> *in such a night*
> *Stood Dido with a willow in her hand*
> *Upon the wild sea-banks, and waft her love*
> *To come again to Carthage.*

This very summer I had heard that magic speech at Stratford, in the theatre by the river where the willows trail their branches in the water. Shakespeare loved them; he must have walked often along those banks and watched the grey-green leaves fluttering in the wind. No weeping willows then, with their golden rain and their allusive name, *Salix babylonica*. They were not yet brought from China. I thought of the whack of bat on leather at Lord's on a summer afternoon, of all the men, from Test captains to village cricketers, who handle bats made from the noble *Salix alba*.

> *Down by the sally gardens,*
> *My love and I did meet.*

Yeats wrote. Sallies, they call them in Ireland, from their generic name, and a sally garden is a willow plantation. There was one I used to walk through down to a deep pool at the bend of a great river where salmon leap, and once, just beyond the sallies, I lay in the dried-up bed of a stream at dusk on a winter evening, listening. to the tender, heart-rending, unearthly voices of a huge flock of curlew on the edge of the floodwater. I know an English stream, with trout in it, where the willows in winter are like flames flickering along the bank in the pale sunlight, and I remember the palm that we used to pick from the goat-Willows, loving its furry touch.

Crack! The branch was sawn through, and a sprinkling of fine white powder lay among the grass and nettles at my feet. Dragging it out, I saw that the sun was going down behind the broken line of willows; the rooks had gone home, the air was chilly, and it was time for tea. Goodnight, old willow. Until to-morrow.

STICKS FOR THE FIRE

W E HAD BEEN having some trees felled and I, with my sense of frugality pleasantly satisfied, was picking up sticks from the areas where the trees had fallen and storing them in the woodshed for kindling the winter's fires. It was late October, a still, golden day when the whole earth seemed hushed and drowsy. 'Like silence listening to silence,' Hood called it. The beech trees were foxy red, the chestnut leaves – such as remained – a flaming yellow, the oaks not yet turned and the elms a patchwork of leaves still green and others already golden. Any night now, a frost would bring a transformation and a great fall and we should see the branches that have been hidden these last six months or so. It is, in a sense, a second spring for when the leaves are gone the tracery of branch and twig, the shapes of such delicate beauty, flower for us once more against the sky as leaf and blossom flowered in the spring.

I had an assortment of sticks to collect and, as I piled them in my arms and carried them to the shed, I amused myself by naming each tree from which they had come and tracing it as far back in memory as I could. This old Bramley apple, wood which would smell sweet burning in the hearth on winter evenings – I had often helped to relieve it of its load. How many thousand apples, I wondered, had it produced in its lifetime, to be stored away in the apple house whose dim interior was scented by the fruit and lightened by the gleam of the waxen skins?

These branches were from an acacia tree in which, many years ago, I found the only tree-creeper's nest I have ever discovered. It was between the trunk and a loose piece of bark, a miracle of neatness and ingenious concealment. I recorded it in the old notebook I kept for just such information. When I found it on May 24, there were four young in it. On June 7 I reported that one of the babies had got squashed but the other three had flown.

I took, on my next journey to the woodshed, an armful of Scotch fir branches – good for starting the fire, but they would crackle and spit and need watching. I saw, with satisfaction, my stick pile growing. Some deep atavistic pleasure lies in the work of harvesting anything, be it corn or apples, blackberries or wood. It comes down to us, no doubt, from our remote ancestors for whom life was a constant struggle against hunger and cold, an unrelenting round of working to harness Nature to help survival. It is not, nowadays, so universal a feeling among country people as it once was. In my childhood it was a common sight to see women out 'wooding', using the pram (as soon as it was vacated by the last occupant) for bringing home the sticks and odd fallen branches that they collected along the roadsides.

Crossing the lawn on my way back from the woodshed to the edge of the orchard, I stood for a moment to look across the little pastoral scene of distant fields opened up by the felling of the trees; such an English scene – lush pasture and fat cattle, the tall elms, the red and gold of what de la Mare called 'the rusting harvest hedgerow', the line of willows along the stream and, in the far distance, the Fosse, now a grassy lane.

A robin came while I was collecting lime branches and sat on a sawn-up pile of logs. He sang a few snatches and was not troubled by the sharp crack of sticks as I held one end under my boot and bent the branch to break it up. I remembered sitting on these logs in the soft twilight of a September evening some six weeks ago. The children had worked hard all afternoon carrying branches to the site, where it had been decided to build a bonfire to dispose of the first crop of rubbish from the fallen trees. A great stack had been built. The wood was dry and the bottom of the stack was cunningly composed of branches from an ancient cupressus tree, highly inflammable.

As twilight came, excitement mounted; everyone was summoned, including the dog, and at last the moment arrived when the match would be struck. It was a magnificent bonfire. I sat on the logs and watched the great flames leaping up and the sparks whirling away into the darkening sky while the children ran to and fro, piling on more wood and calling directions to each other. Long before the end it was quite dark, but in the light from the flames we could see one another's faces, illuminated and a little unreal. It was somehow symbolic, that bonfire, as though the long hot summer and the happy holidays so soon to end were going out in a blaze of glory. The scar remains on the ground, but long after the grass has grown over it again we shall remember that evening.

Now it would soon be evening again – an earlier one. The sun was getting low in the sky and as I gathered up my last load there ran in my head the lines of a song from long ago:

> *Summer is gone,*
> *October twilight*
> *Steals through my skylight*
> *At the close of the day.*

Summer is gone; winter lies ahead with frost and fogs and journeys on slippery roads, yet with its own peculiar beauty – sunlight on snow, ice patterns on the windows, bare, silent woods, and long evenings beside the fire, where each piece of wood that burns is an old familiar friend.

THE PLEASURES OF STONEWALLING

T IS A DRY-STONE WALL, about six feet high, which divides the garden from the wood-yard. A violent gale in late November tore a boat-shaped hole in it, the base of which – not much above ground-level – was wide enough for a tall man to lie down in, and the sides of which slanted outwards to a width of some ten or twelve feet.

I had watched dry-stone walling being done and, having grasped the theory, had long hankered after trying my hand at it. So when I announced that the wall had blown down, I added that it would be rather fun to try to build it up again. I said it as one sometimes says it would be fun to go to Tibet or learn to write with one's toes, and if the remark had gone unchallenged I should probably never have become an amateur stone-mason. But immediately everybody assured me that it was a highly skilled job, not to be undertaken without long experience, and I was offered a two shillings bet against finishing it by the end of the year. I accepted the bet and made up my mind to build that wall if I burst in the attempt.

I first cleared away the fallen stones from the base of the wall, sorting them roughly into two heaps – large and small. Then the leaning and insecure bits that remained had to be pulled down so that a good, firm base was left to work on and there was no danger of the sides collapsing further. Then I was ready to begin.

I worked slowly, choosing each stone with care and constantly reminding myself of the principles of building a wall. Each course, or layer, must be kept flat, the outer stones, which form the wall-face, perfectly flush with the course below, and the joints between stones should never come directly above each other in successive courses, as this weakens the wall. The middle must be filled up with small stones and chips packed in tightly and carefully so that all the chinks are filled up and no stone will rock or shift if touched. Ashes are helpful as a filling, as they will settle in the crevices and then set hard, but a good supply of small stones should suffice. After laying three or four courses, it is advisable to use some stones big enough to reach right across the wall, from one face to the other, and to repeat this process at intervals. These are called tie-stones, as they hold the two faces together. A string held taut along the length of the wall by two sticks is a useful indication of the desirable straight line, but in any case it is essential to stand back and look from afar now and again, as otherwise a slant in the line of each layer or in the vertical line of the wall-face may become exaggerated. Two or three hours' work without these pauses to take stock may be fatal.

Such were the rules that I tried to follow. To begin with they did not always work out. The first two courses were certainly not horizontal, but after that they began to look better. I sloped the two wall-faces slightly in towards each other for greater firmness, but soon realised that I was overdoing it and that if the slope continued the top of the wall would be the breadth of a hair. So I straightened it out. But the thing was not as difficult as they had told me. It was like doing a jigsaw puzzle or packing a suitcase, and anyone who can do either can certainly build a wall. The point at which I had started to build was marked by the abrupt ending of the moss that covered the stones below, so that I could measure at a glance how much it had grown since I began. The fascination of steadily increasing the layers of stone above that high-water mark of moss was enthralling. I was able to work only intermittently, but I thought about it when I was away from the wall and I slunk off to it at all sorts of odd moments when I should have been doing something else, telling myself I would work for just ten minutes and then staying there much longer, completely absorbed. It was the joy of the child with his bricks, the poet with his verses, the sculptor with his marble, the joy of making out of formless material something that has form and significance.

Working away in the grey December afternoons towards Christmas, I used to think about the people that had built this wall before, about how long it had stood and how much longer it would stand. I thought about the million walls that chequer the bare, sweeping uplands of the Cotswolds and the many hands that built them with this same golden stone. I thought how strange it is that history records the names of architects, but never of the men that skilfully lay stone upon stone to give life to the architect's vision. Sometimes I hummed Christmas carols as I lifted and turned the stones this way and that to fit them. A robin sang sometimes a little snatch of its sad, gentle song from the prunus tree; down in the wood a jay screeched in frequent indignation, and the pigeons flopped in to roost as the light faded.

By Christmas the wall had reached a height of 4 ft., and there it seemed to stick. After hours of work it looked no bigger. I suddenly wanted to give up the whole thing but, funking the loss of face, I went on. On Boxing Day I saw that it was perceptibly larger and the heaps of stones were smaller. I knew those stones, then, as a shepherd knows his sheep, and I found myself picking, unerringly, the one that was the right shape for the gap I must fill. From then on it went well, in spite of my having to use steps to reach the top, which slowed me down. The last day of the old year dawned upon a wall still incomplete, but I knew by then that I had made it. I put on the last stone five minutes before lunchtime and went to draw my two shillings.

My experience as a mason has left its mark. I shall never, I think, admire a Gloucestershire landscape so carelessly again. And when following hounds, the day after the work was finished, I saw somebody jump a stone wall

and knock off the two top courses, I strangled with
difficulty my cry of anguish.

THE POPLARS ARE FELLED

T HE CREOSOTE that I was painting on to the
abbreviated tree-trunks smelled unpleasant, and
bits of sawdust kept sticking to my brush. It was a
tiresome job, the more so because it was necessitated by the
felling of the two Lombardy poplars that have stood before
the house through three generations of occupants and were
fully grown even before that occupancy began.

As I dabbled my brush over the soft white wood, I
composed in my mind a sort of obituary of these trees.
'Populus Nigra. Born at – one knows not where. Planted, one
may surmise, some 70 years ago.' It is not possible to be
precise about the date. Our oldest inhabitant is 91 but spent
her early years in alien territory all of five miles away, while
the octogenarian who comes next in seniority has only been
here for 60 years. So no one now living in this community

saw the planting of the poplars. It must, however, have been co-incidental with the removal of the old farm buildings and the re-planning of the whole area where they had stood.

Three years ago, they began, in unison, to look sickly, and their foliage became noticeably thin. The following summer it was worse – a few green tufts on the ends of some of the branches was all that they could manage. Last year they were plainly and indubitably dead. Since they stood directly in front of one building and within perhaps fifteen yards of another, we contemplated with dismay the difficulties of felling them. There was talk of getting them down in sections, and one imagined a hideous bill. They seemed, for the moment, safe enough, and we decided to leave them.

In winter, when they would be bare anyway, one could almost forget that they were dead. One could still look from the window on a clear, frosty night and see them with the moon behind. Even better, one could see the rising sun touch them on a frosty morning when their poor, dead limbs were covered with rime and gave back such an answering sparkle and glitter that there seemed still to be life there.

But with the coming of spring, pretence was no longer possible. Their beauty then was only a memory – a memory that assailed me sharply now as I moved round the trunk, working my creosote brush into the crevices. On spring mornings how often have I leaned from the window to watch the play of light and shadow in the restlessly stirring leaves. Gerard Manley Hopkins, mourning the felling of some poplars that he had known and loved, described how their 'airy cages quelled, Quelled or quenched in leaves the leaping sun'.

And the Rev. Francis Kilvert, that incomparable diarist, wrote: 'For some time I have been trying to find the right word for the shimmering, glancing, twinkling movement of the poplar leaves in the sun and wind. This afternoon I saw the word written on the poplar leaves. It was 'dazzle''

On summer nights when all was still there would be always the faint rustling of the poplars. I read somewhere once of a blind man who said that he could tell what sort of tree he stood beside simply by the differing sounds the leaves made. If this astonishing feat is possible it is more easily believed of the sound of poplars for their leaves move quite differently from those of any other tree. Housman recalled their sound in one of the most poignant poems of exile ever written. He remembered, in his loneliness in London, the country where he was born and the poplars by some nameless brook.

> *There, in the windless night-time,*
> *The wanderer, marvelling why,*
> *Halts on the bridge to hearken*
> *How soft the poplars sigh.*

On April evenings a song-thrush would often choose one of these trees from which to sing its final song of the day. Tree-creepers loved their bark and would travel up them with quick, jerky movements, probing for food with their needle-like beaks. Once – glorious memory – four crossbills spent a whole day in these two trees, nipping off the leaves and scattering them on the ground. It was my first – and only – sight of these birds. Next morning they were gone.

One day a man rang our door-bell. He was a peripatetic tree-feller, had seen the dead trees and suggested he might have the job. There was a conference, an agreement and immediate action. A rope, a chain-saw and a hand-saw were fetched from his truck and his two assistants were mobilised. Holding the rope coiled in his hand, Joe went up the first tree like a monkey, cutting the side branches as he went. At the half-way mark he stopped and tied the rope securely round the tree. How, I wondered, would he get down again with no foot-holds left? But it was quite simple; he slid down the rope. He went up again by the same route with the chain-saw slung round him and cut a wedge from the trunk, a white wound in the tree's side. Then, with his mates pulling on the rope in the required direction, he cut through the trunk. There was a splintering crash and the top of the tree lay on the ground.

Within two hours both trees were down, leaving the two 4 ft-high stumps that I had now finished creosoting. They will serve as posts for climbing shrubs that will soon cover them. I put away the creosote and went in to consult the nursery catalogues.

SEPTEMBER SONG

I USED TO HAVE a rough timetable by which, when the holidays were over and the children departed I turned my attention to the garden. Perhaps it was a sort of consolation when there were no longer pounding feet on the stairs and music issuing from open windows. After the Christmas holidays, it was the seed order, and after the summer holidays it was the general stocktaking with notebook and pencil, looking at this year's shrubs and considering what next. Upon this pleasant task I would walk, as I was walking now, along the path between the rows of stone pillars which support the gnarled and aged wistaria. But I no longer had my notebook for the garden is now the responsibility of the next generation and my mind holds only memories.

There is a moment in September when one is suddenly aware that summer is on the wane and autumn is arriving. The butterflies still flicker over the buddleia and the sedum and the sun is still warm, but the light has changed, becoming more mellow, more deeply golden, the rooks are clamorous but with different voices from those of spring, and there is a smell in the air, an indefinable something that is autumn.

To us in the English countryside our lives are so bound up with the pattern of the changing seasons that one can scarcely imagine what it must be like to live in equatorial lands where there is neither summer nor winter. What an impoverishment of life! For, as one grows older, there is an added importance to seasonal change in that each season becomes to some extent redolent of the emotions and experiences that we have passed through in other years. Thus, spring, with its wild, restless energy driving the sap up through the branches, with the chiff-chaff calling and the husky-voiced cuckoo, recalls a childhood and a garden and the vaguely disturbing high ambitions of youth, and a 1ong hot summer will always be, to those of us who lived through it, tinged by the recollection of 1940 and the anxious watch from every hilltop for the German parachutists. Thus, too, a winter snowfall brings back a time of siege, surrounded by blocked roads, happily spent in writing, hour after hour, day after day, before a 1og fire, and the triumph of wa1king out on to the crisp snow in the bright sunshine and exulting that the book was finished. Every winter is the sum of all our winters – those of content and discontent.

But perhaps it is most of all September – the watershed between summer and autumn – that brings back, unbidden, the ghost of past emotions. The little, thin, sad song of the robin and the sharp, fresh smell of the mornings when the dew lies thick, never fail to remind me of the dread and terror of an inexorably approaching first departure of myself to boarding school, of often repeated efforts at self-comfort, 'It can't happen, it can't happen.' But, of course, it did, and the unhappiness that followed was deep and real enough to be the material, after many years, of a recurring nightmare. From the path under the wistaria, I could look up to the window at which, so long ago, I had aired myself after a very hot bath in the hope that pneumonia might save me from the approaching fate. (But not even a cold ensued.)

Now I contemplated the deserted swimming pool beside which the glorious red rose Sympathie had come well through the summer despite the drought. In my mind I heard the laughter and voices not only of my children but also of *their* children, recently departed, in their turn, back to their schools but without, thank God, dread or terror. September still means name-tapes and trunks and the hasty pursuit of forgotten bits of uniform, but I am on the other side of two fences now, not homesick but feeling bereft by the absence. I remembered what joy there had been in the hot summer days – splashes and shouts, brown limbs coasting through the water, prints of wet feet on the concrete. There comes back to me especially, one night of full moon when it was still – at 10 o'clock – a pleasure (for some) to seek the coolness of the water. The underwater light was turned on, giving a sort of unreality to the supple bodies leaping from the diving-board in a curve like a leaping salmon in reverse. The swifts had finished their happy screaming round the house and gone to sleep; only the bats circled and flickered above us. 'On such a night . . '. It was a moment isolated in time, never to be forgotten, a jewel to be carefully preserved in the cotton wool of memory.

I went back under the tunnel of wistaria on to the lawn where cracks in the ground still gaped after the drought. Here, too, I could recall the figures of long ago – the girl spread- eagled in the hot sun and the boy setting off across the orchard, with his gun under his arm and the Labrador at his heels, to shoot pigeons. There came into my mind the lines of a song from the past:

> *And the autumn frosts*
> *Turn the leaves to flame,*
> *And I haven't got time*
> *For the waiting game.*

Time – what is this great mystery? An invention, one may say, of man with his clocks and calendars. Yet it is real enough and our faces register it more surely than the face of a clock. The autumn frosts come and go, the leaves die and are reborn, the seed is planted and ripens to harvest; sunrise and sunset, waxing and waning moon, bud and blossom and fruit. Two generations lie between the young girl at the

window trying to get pneumonia and the young people –
no longer children – leaping from the quiet moonlit garden
into the lighted water of the swimming pool; yet it is
nothing. Nothing more than the length of a poem or the
coursing of water from the mountain spring to the river
estuary. It is only in youth that we imagine that time is our
servant. None of us can stay for the 'waiting game'.

THE OBITUARY OF A PEN

I THINK I WAS ELEVEN when the pen was given to me. it
was not my first fountain pen, and the sight of the
blue and brown mottled barrel lying in its slim box
gave me satisfaction but no special thrill. Anyhow, I began
to use it straight away. I inscribed my name with it – in a
still childish handwriting – in a book of European history
that I still have in my bookshelves. When I was fourteen, it
went to boarding school with me and there we became

closer to each other in the process of writing frequent and extremely long letters home, the only alleviation of my more-or-less perpetual homesickness.

I began then to write poetry – bad poetry, hut deeply felt – and after I had left school I decided to try submitting a poem for publication in *The Field*. Not knowing at all how to set about it, I typed out my poem and then wrote – with Old Mottley of course – a humble but impassioned appeal to the Editor to publish it. It was wartime, and I was working then in the office of the local Home Guard, travelling the four miles to work every day on my bicycle. For several days I pedalled home at extra speed to see if there was an answer from *The Field*. At last, one day, it was there. The editor was very interested and sympathetic but pointed out that I had forgotten to enclose the poem. It was a humiliation for me and for Old Mottley. We hurriedly sent it off, with an apology, and a kind note came back saying that it was unsuitable.

Soon afterwards, my pen went with me to London to work in the Foreign Office. There it had a busy time, working in the office by day and, in the evening, writing experimental drafts of stories, essays and poems. The feel of it in my hand had now begun to he a part of putting thought into words. I no longer liked to fill it but had formed the habit of using the pauses while words took shape to dip it and to dip it again.

The final perfection was given to Old Mottley by a young man called Robin who worked in my office. One day I dropped my pen and he trod on it which gave to the nib a more excellent shape even than it had possessed before. Robin was going to be a missionary in China. I wonder what strange territory his foot has trodden since it trod on Old Mottley. Further, the thought occurs to me that he was a Protestant Ulsterman and, in view of the fact that, some sixteen years later, Old Mottley would be writing to my friends and relations to announce my reception into the Catholic Church, I wonder if there was something prophetic and symbolic about the descent of that large foot.

I was still in the Foreign Office when Old Mottley wrote the first short story that I was to have published, and, soon after that, during a long sick leave occasioned by jaundice, Mottley and I set to work on our first novel. It was extraordinary how we understood each other. As the good rider is said to be part of his horse, so the good pen is part of the writer. Old Mottley was like an extension of my hand, connected directly with my brain.

It was at about that time that a sudden fear gripped me about what would happen if I lost Mottley. I felt prudence required me to insure against this hideous possibility, so I went to a shop that sold only that brand of pen and asked them if they could find a nib similar to mine which I could keep in reserve. They gave me several to try – all hopeless. Finally, they said that they were sorry but my nib was so bent and twisted from its original shape that they could not produce anything like it. Robin's foot had done its work.

The years passed. Mottley and I wrote more books, some short stories, some articles and countless letters. It was with Mottley that I answered my husband's proposal of marriage, with Mottley that I announced my engagement to friends, and it should have been with Mottley that I signed the marriage register but a wedding dress is not really meant for carrying a pen so my new name was signed for the first time with a borrowed plume. But Mottley, of course, came on our honeymoon to Spain, wrote the first letters from our first house, and announced the impending arrival of our son and then our daughter. It recorded in 'the children's book' the first tooth cut, the first step taken, the early words and phrases. And Mottley, by then some twenty-five years old, may have been grateful for the fact that, through these years of preoccupation with the children, work for him diminished. But he continued a perfect servant, and, somehow, I had come to believe that he was indestructible. I had ceased to wonder how I was going to write when I no longer had him.

Then, one day, as I was writing a letter, suddenly and without warning, one of the twin points of the nib snapped off. Desperate, I took Mottley to London and asked the shop to despatch him to the makers and tell them to fit a nib as like as possible to the broken one. I knew it would not be the same – indeed, dreadfully, horribly different – but at least I should still have the familiar feel of the barrel in my hand. And perhaps some obliging person would tread on it for me; this time, I thought I would ask a Catholic. A week later, the still mutilated Mottley returned to me. 'We are sorry,' the accompanying note said, 'that this model is obsolete and it is not possible to fit a new nib'.

So that was the end. But, of course, he still lives in the pen-tray on my desk so that when ideas refuse to flow or there is something momentous to say I can hold him in my hand and go through the motions of writing. Sometimes it helps.

A RIVER FOR ALL SEASONS

T HE FIRST TIME I made the journey from Rosslare to Ballyduff in the friendly little train that stopped at every station, I did not know the engine driver, nor even that his name was Mr Bolster. But later I was to get used to waving to him if I saw the train pass in the morning or – as was more usual – on the return journey in the afternoon when it was going to connect with the boat back to Fishguard.

Over the years, I was to come to know well that enchanted valley of the Blackwater, the hillsides in spring covered with great splashes of yellow gorse like spilled egg-yolk, the villages of little colour-washed houses, the Knockmealdown Mountains blue with distance and the deep salmon pools where Bartholomew Flynn – known to all as Batt – instructed, cajoled, advised, criticised and sometimes praised those who pitted their wits against the king of fish.

I was to know it from several angles, geographically speaking, for my base was sometimes south of the river, up on the hill, sometimes north of it, across the valley, and sometimes in Ballyduff itself. There I was often awakened in the morning by the fearsome noise of an ass braying, and from my window I could see and hear the life of the village going on in what Batt sarcastically called 'O'Connell Street, Ballyduff'. Only a couple of doors away was the Post Office where Mrs Bolger sold stamps, sweets, groceries, shoes, saucepans and almost anything else one could think of, as well as presiding over the telephone exchange which was a cause of much shouting and confusion but which – on the rare occasions when it worked – proved a rich source of gossip. On the other side of the street was Murphy's store where Mick Murphy, who was a big man, often found himself short of space and so could be seen unrolling and measuring lengths of linoleum along the pavement outside.

The bridge over the river was at the end of the village street and near it stood the ugly little church which was the centre of Ballyduff's life. Thither to Mass in the morning and Benediction in the evening went the devout on weekdays and the whole village on Sundays, and when the bell rang the Angelus at noon and at six o'clock everything stopped in Ballyduff.

Through all my memories of the valley the river runs – the river in every season, in foul weather as well as fair, in low water or in spate. The names of its reaches and pools come back to my mind – the Twigyard, Kilmurry, the Weir Pool – places where I have watched duck flying overhead or a solitary heron sitting hunched on the bank and heard the liquid call of the curlew. At Lower Carysville, between Fermoy and Ballyduff, the river runs close to the road, a stretch of deep, smooth water. A row of white poplars stood along the bank, reflected in the surface, and the play of the wind turned the leaves to and fro, showing now their darker, now their whiter side.

There was a favourite pool for salmon near the great swirling bend in the river called Tobin's Hole. An iron gate from the road led into the field that one must traverse to reach it, and opposite the gate stood a little whitewashed cabin. The old woman who lived there had a local reputation for the evil eye and was known as 'the pishogue'. On fishing days Batt would approach the iron gate cautiously, watching over his shoulder all the time to see if the pishogue would appear. If she did, the day was finished. ''Tis no good at all' he would say with conviction. 'We'll not be catching a fish today on account of the look she gave us.'

In spring the valley was at its most beautiful, a landscape of wonderfully lush green fields with clumps of primroses blooming under the hedges. I remember especially one evening driving along the road from Kilworth to Ballyduff and coming to a little ruined church. I went into the churchyard and stood among the sloping, weather-beaten gravestones with a breeze from the Atlantic blowing cold and clean on my face. Ivy had grown thickly over the ruined walls, covering compassionately their jagged edges, and time had wiped away the names written on the stones. Even such bitter sorrows as these people had endured must fade at last.

The light was going rapidly and all the sky was a soft grey except for an orange streak in the west. I went back slowly through the long grass, wet with dew, and out on to the road. A donkey cart was passing, carrying a load of turf, and the man who drove it gave me 'Good night'. The 'click, click' of the donkey's hoofs died away as the first star appeared and the road lay before me, silent, white and empty.

SHOPPING IN A KERRY VILLAGE

I T IS A NEAT little village. Round the four sides of what is grandly called North Square stand colour-washed houses: blue, pink, white, green. Beyond it the river flows past the church and the rest of the village straggles away eastwards until it peters out, leaving the road to travel on between the great wide expanses of peat bogs. The little white cabins away in the distance are the outliers of the village. The inhabitants come in to Mass on Sundays, bring a calf to the monthly market and visit Casey's Bar of an evening. The fact that they are two or three miles away does not mean that they are not intimately acquainted with the affairs of everyone in the village, just as their own fortunes, courtships and illnesses (human and animal) are known in North Square. It is a small world over which the great hills of Kerry brood, and what happens beyond them has not much reality.

There are five or six shops, mostly offering the same sort of goods but some with a bigger stock than others. Under one roof one can find sweets, pullovers, scarves, boots, rugs, fruit, ashtrays, postcards. On our first visit there it was an Aran pullover we sought for an 11-year-old girl. There was some difficulty in finding the right size. The first shop had larger ones and smaller ones but nothing that

was right. 'Will I go up to Mrs. O'Reilly for ye and see if she
has one?' the proprietor asked.

We thanked her and said we would go ourselves. I
stayed to buy some apples, and the eager searcher hurried
on to the next shop. When I emerged I was not sure where
to look for her. I entered a shop farther along the street,
which had an array of pullovers in the window. An old lady
stood behind the counter. 'Has a little girl been in to ask for
an Aran pullover?' I inquired.

'She's not; but will you have a sweet?' and she pushed
towards me a big glass jar of humbugs. How could one
refuse such a kindly invitation? Then my eye lighted upon a
cheeseboard, shaped like a table-tennis bat, hanging from a
shelf. On it was a shamrock and the words 'A Present from
Sneem'. I thought immediately of a benevolent headmaster
who administers light-handed justice to the behinds of his
boys with a wooden spoon. How much better, I thought, to
be whacked for talking after lights out by A Present from
Sneem. So I bought it. ''Tis fine for the cheese', the old lady
said as she wrapped it up. I agreed, and felt rather deceitful.
We talked of the village, of the beauty of the countryside, of
the years that she had lived there – all her life. 'My husband
died last winter. God rest his soul.' She crossed herself. I,
too, said a prayer for the repose of his soul. She wiped away
a tear with the back of her hand, and we each had another
humbug. We parted with promises of an early reunion.

Outside in the street I found the children, one already
wearing triumphantly the Aran pullover. It is good for the
women who make them in their scattered homes that they

have become so popular, but a little sad to see so many
foreign tourists wearing them with no idea of their history.
The complicated patterns of them are peculiar to each
family – like the tartan of the Highlander – and are handed
down from mother to daughter.

The children departed to another shop, and I
wandered through the square and stood leaning on the
bridge, looking down at the river. A grey wagtail alighted on
a rock, flirting its tail, and flew away again. A few rings
spread slowly from rising fish in the pool downstream. The
air was full of the scent of peat smoke; the gorse was in
bloom and lay in great golden patches across the
countryside, and the cloud shadows moved slowly over the
hillsides.

I remembered suddenly my first visit to an Irish
village shop, years ago in the enchanted valley of the
Blackwater. That shop had been also the post office, and I
had had some reason to make a telephone call to Dublin.
Mrs. Quin could not have been more disconcerted if I had
asked her to get Moscow. There was a lot of turning of the
handle at the side of her ancient machine and shouting into
it. Then there was a long wait during which I sat in the
corner of the shop on a sack of potatoes and watched the
customers come in and listened to the conversation. The
telephone rang and everyone announced that it must be my
call to Dublin, but it was not.

Mrs. Quin held the telephone to her ear and listened,
breathless; then she put it down and crossed herself. 'God
help us!' she exclaimed. I did not quite like to ask what had

happened. A grave illness? A death in the family? The speculations were ended when she called upstairs to her daughter, 'Kitty, the Inspector is coming. He's just left Lismore.' 'Oh my God,' cried Kitty, 'where's the book? How many stamps was it Mick had this morning and we telling him to leave paying till another time?'

I always regretted that my call to Dublin came before the Inspector, so that I missed his visit. I hope Mrs. Quin did not get into trouble for the deficiencies of her book-keeping. She was a kindly soul.

There remained one purchase to make in Sneem – from the chemist. His shop had a more sophisticated look than any other, but to our surprise we found it locked. 'Try the blue door,' said a man passing by. ''That's his house. He's maybe not up yet.' It was 11.30 a.m. Perhaps he was ill. We rang the bell and the chemist appeared wearing his bedroom slippers. He was delighted to see us, unlocked the shop and provided our wants. We asked after his health. He said it was grand. Later, we asked, very tactfully, one of the local inhabitants why the chemist was up so late. 'Oh, he's a great man for reading. A very learned man. He'll read till two or three in the morning. He had a shop in Waterville, but there was too much business; it kept him from his reading. So he gave it up and came here where 'tis quieter.'

I thought about it that evening, looking at the sea and listening to the gentle sucking surge of the waves and the cries of oyster-catchers. I looked at the hills, purple hued and shadowed at the day's ending – the old, patient, compassionate hills that dwarf all human endeavour, all human ambition – and I wondered if perhaps the chemist of Sneem had not got the answer to life.

UNBIDDEN AT AN IRISH WEDDING

ALLINTUBBER ABBEY' the signpost said, in the green lettering used in Ireland to denote a place of historic interest. We stopped the car and considered whether to follow it. The small and inadequate guidebook that I had bought hurriedly in Dublin before we headed for the west made no mention of it, but the little road looked inviting and we decided to take it.

We had motored, that morning, through Joyce's country up to Louisburgh and along the edge of Clew Bay. It was a day of alternating storms and sunshine. Sometimes, for a few minutes, the landscape was blotted out by driving rain which would clear suddenly, opening to us a wide view, breathtakingly beautiful, of moorland and bog, green and brown, purpled with heather and stretching away to the blue hills. The fuchsia hedges were in bloom along the sides of the roads and round the gardens in front of the little whitewashed cabins, and clumps of montbretia made vivid orange splashes at the edge of the streams. The roads were almost deserted: sometimes we met a donkey cart bringing in a load of turf; once every ten miles or so, we met a car. On one of the stretches of moorland we stopped and walked for a time, savouring the silence. Now and then there was the call of a curlew or the distant voice of a sheep; otherwise nothing. It was a silence beyond the mere absence of noise; it was something positive, something that one could hear. Beside Clew Bay we had watched parties of waders feeding on the wet mud uncovered by the receding tide. Some cormorants stood in a solemn black line, staring into space; oyster-catchers rose hurriedly from just below the road and flew away seawards, uttering their loud, liquid call.

Now, as we drove along the lane to Ballintubber, a rapidly approaching black cloud promised us another downpour. The abbey stands beside the road, a small romanesque building, part of it without a roof but part restored in modern times. The storm began just as we were leaving the car, and we ran, cowering into our macintoshes, to the door. A wedding had just taken place and the couple were in the sacristy with the priest while the wedding guests sat waiting. The young man at the harmonium was playing, most appropriately, Handel's Water Music. We crept to a back seat and sat down to contemplate the splendid simplicity of the rough-cut stone walls, the vaulted roof, the four single-light windows above the altar. On each side of the chancel, in the transepts, were two tiny side-chapels.

The young man at the harmonium stopped playing and there was a silence; we could hear a murmur of voices from the sacristy where the bride and bridegroom waited for the rain to cease before they made their exit. The congregation shuffled a bit and there were some whispers. The men were uncomfortable in their dark suits and white collars, the women a little self-conscious in their best hats. Suddenly there was a splash somewhere just in front of us. The harmonium player looked up at the leaking roof, then down at the drop of water which had landed a few inches from him, and then looked away. Minutes passed; there was another splash, and then another. With a sigh, the young man rose, lifted the harmonium bodily 6 ft. to the right, set his chair before it, and sat down again.

Outside the rain still poured down. I looked up at the vaulted chancel roof. Here, before this same altar, for 700 years and through bitter persecution, despite the edicts of Henry VIII and the destructions of Oliver Cromwell, priest after priest, down through the generations, had said Mass. Terrible dramas had centred on this building, blind hatreds, tragic misunderstandings, deep faith, courageous loyalty. Now, thank God, those hatreds are dead. There was a sudden lessening of the hiss and patter of the rain outside. One of the guests opened the door to look out, reported. an improvement, and hurried to the sacristy to tell the good news. The young man at the harmonium prepared for action, the congregation stirred, attention turned towards the doors of the sacristy. The Wedding March sounded, the bridal couple came down the aisle and passed out of the north door. The guests followed.

At the little chapel of St. Joseph, I said a prayer for the young couple whose names we should never know. How strange, I reflected, are life's chance meetings – like the little white roads that cross the bog to meet once and part again for ever. One day, probably, these two will bring their children here for christening; and some day, old and grey, they will themselves be brought to lie here while their requiem is sung. And they will never know that for two people, far away across the Irish Sea, the name of Ballintubber will always recall their wedding day.

On our way home that evening we had a puncture just outside a little farm. The woman of the house came out with some scraps for the hens and stood to watch us change the wheel. We talked. She had always lived here, she said, but her sister had married 'away.' I thought of England, or perhaps the United. States, and enquired where. 'Cong,' she. said. It was all of five miles from where we stood. She looked with interest at our car. 'Cortina,' she read out. 'Ah, I've heard of them. There's a terrible speed on them.'

When the wheel was changed, we bade her goodbye and drove away. Our puncture would be a story to tell her husband that evening; our car, perhaps, a source of dreams for her, a link with the outside world. And for us there were dreams, too – of blue mountains, fuchsia hedges, and the candles burning in the dimness of Ballintubber Abbey.

A SHELL FROM THE GALICIAN SHORE

THE GALICIAN SHORE, upon which the notorious Atlantic rollers broke with remarkable gentleness, was quite deserted. For as far as one could see – perhaps a mile – the only life, the only movement, was of bird and plant and wave. Lying on the sand in the delicious heat of that sun of which one had dreamed through so many cold, grey summer days in England, I watched idly through my binoculars a party of greenshank feeding high up on the shore. One of them, uninterested, dozed, standing on one leg; the others worked steadily over the ground, moving elegantly on their long, thin legs and bending gracefully to probe the sand with their long, thin beaks.

Behind us – 40 miles inland – was Santiago de Compostela, which we had left the previous day. It would be wrong to call our visit there a pilgrimage since such a journey essentially suggests something of the penitential, which was not to be found in our luxurious hotel. Within its walls, it is true, pilgrims had dwelt from the time of Ferdinand and Isabella onwards, but they were not surrounded by the present splendid furnishings nor fed by the present delicious food. Something of a pilgrimage, however, it had been, for the penitential element was present in the journey across the Bay of Biscay when we were prostrated by sea-sickness, and we had gone daily, across the magnificent square, to the Cathedral to pray at the tomb of St. James.

The emblem of St. James and of the pilgrims to his shrine is the cockleshell. The legend is that when the saint's body was being brought from Palestine to Spain, where earlier he had preached the gospel, a man on horseback was miraculously saved from drowning in the sea as the boat bearing St. James's body passed. The man and his horse emerged from the waves covered in cockleshells. The shell is seen everywhere in Santiago – exquisitely sculptured on doorways, roughly cut on walls, fashioned by the silver-smiths into spoons and ashtrays. And here on the seashore, where our pilgrimage ended, we had come to idle away a few days in the sun, and we met, again and again, the cockleshells of the legend.

Like the lazy greenshank, I dozed for a time, lulled by the sound of the sea, the thump of the waves breaking and the whisper of their withdrawal – bewitching noise that speaks both of time and eternity. I roused myself to see a tern fly past and, shutting its wings, plummet down like a stone to fall into the sea with a splash. A moment later it was up and away again, its quarry seized.

We set out to walk along the beach, stopping now and then to look at birds or to pick up some particularly beautiful shell to take home to the children in England. A party of sanderlings were feeding along the tide-line: fat, endearing little birds that ran after each receding wave with a rapid, waddling gait. Suddenly we saw, lying on the sand a few yards clear of the sea, the biggest shell I have ever seen. It was what is called, I think, a conch shell, about eight inches long from tip to tip, whitish in colour near the base but, where it swelled outwards to its thickest part, chequered with an exquisite pattern of browns and blacks. The inhabitant, we found, was still inside, which was a drawback to our plan to take it home with us. I collected a piece of driftwood and, with this, poked at the grey, rubbery-looking contents of the shell. It withdrew with a dissatisfied sucking noise. I tried a flanking movement with the bit of wood but without success. Obviously I was not going to move the shell-dweller that way and would probably break the shell. Perhaps someone at the hotel would know how to tackle the job. We set off for home, carrying our treasure gingerly in a towel.

Our way lay through a pine wood, and there were a number of women there with little handcarts busily collecting fallen pine branches to use as winter bedding for their cows. One of them, with cart laden, stood aside on the path to let us pass and we exchanged greetings. She was a good-looking woman with a strong, almost masculine face, big dark eyes and a square, sturdy body matched to her destiny of hard work and child-bearing. With inadequate Spanish augmented by sign language we began a conversation, and she, smiling broadly, was delighted to talk. She had, she told us, four cows and one was sick. Her husband was a fisherman and her eldest son was working in a bank in Barcelona. She signified by that international gesture of thumb and index finger that he was getting good pay. Had she been to Barcelona? She shook her head. She had never left Galicia. At this point I opened the beach towel in which I was carrying the shell and showed it to her. 'Ah,' she exclaimed with interest, 'un comida.'

Since I knew the word meant a meal I was slightly surprised, but supposed the shell's inhabitant to be a special delicacy. I indicated that this was not what we wanted. 'Para los ninos in Inglaterra,' I said, tapping the shell. 'Ah, para los ninos!' She understood, at once, our difficulty and with much nodding and promises of returning in a 'momentito' she took the shell and went off through the trees to the little cabin which was her home leaving us to mind the cart. A few minutes later, she returned, displaying the empty shell. We never knew how she did it, but the result was eminently satisfactory; she had her 'comida' and we had our shell.

We have not, like the pilgrims in the Middle Ages, put a cockleshell above our door to show that we have been to Santiago, but our chequered conch shell has a place of honour on the nursery mantelpiece.

SOUVENIR FROM RHODES

I N THE WARM SUNSHINE of an April day, we sat at the edge of an orange grove on the island of Rhodes, drinking ouzo. The little house from which our drink had come proclaimed itself a café, but there was no one else present, the road was deserted and all was complete peace. The ripe fruit had not yet been picked from the orange grove, and its brilliant colour was complemented by the glossy, dark-green foliage and the blue sky behind. The air was fragrant with blossom, since, apparently, the trees bear again in autumn.

From a stone wall bordering the café's little garden appeared the largest lizard I had ever seen, about eight inches long. Frightened by some movement, he whipped out of sight with alacrity – the flick of a tongue across a dry mouth. Presently he ventured to put his head out and look at us. His wizened face seemed full of the knowledge of some evil older than mankind, which enabled him to regard us with the contempt of an ancient and disillusioned roué for those who have not yet learned the ways of the world. He remained watching us, moving his head slightly from side to side, until we got up to leave.

We drove on along the western coast road, then turned inland, passing through a few small villages. Quite often we met a donkey cart laden with freshly picked oranges and lemons, and sometimes there would be a little stall by the roadside where the fruit was offered for sale. As the car climbed the twisting road through pine woods that smelled delicious in the hot sun, we glimpsed, through breaks in the trees, the blue sea and the distant hills of Turkey.

We stopped to eat our picnic where there were juniper bushes and thyme, a profusion of helianthemums, blue anemones, little white cyclamen and – most exciting of all – a flower that at first glance I took to be a violet. When I came closer I saw that it was a tiny iris, about two inches high, with delicate yellow patterning on its petals. Bending to examine it, I heard what is, to me, a most English sound: the sweet, husky voice of a cuckoo. It was my first hearing that spring, and no one would yet have heard it in England.

Why, I wondered, should it seem so English, since the cuckoo is a summer visitor all over Europe? Perhaps because I have been in other countries that it visits only before its arrival or after its song is finished, and because its voice is woven into my childhood and takes me back, instantly, to cowslips and lush, green grass, and may-blossom powdering the hedgerows.

Every season in our lives is the sum of all the others that have gone before, and the cuckoo in spring will now always be to me not only childhood in England but also April in Rhodes. I had been saved from vaguely arrogating to my native land that beautiful voice; it would have been chauvinism like that of an Englishwoman I remember at a summer luncheon party. Complacently, as she poured out the cream, she said: 'How delicious strawberries are! Do they grow them anywhere except in England?'

Our return journey took us through the village of Ebonas, where two women sat sewing outside a house. On the wall behind them, obviously displayed for sale, hung several gaily-coloured mats. We wanted one for that room usually described in house–agents' advertisements as 'gents' cloaks'. We stopped and asked the price. The women signed to us to wait while one of them hurried off to fetch 'Tia', who was evidently the linguist of the family.

Tia arrived rapidly, beaming and flashing a golden tooth. She was probably quite young but, being married and not in her first youth, she wore the black dress and headscarf that becomes the uniform of the peasant woman long before old age. Her English was not remarkably good but she managed to convey the price, which was extremely low. We chose our mat, in cheerful colours of red and brown, and then she took us to an outhouse to see the loom on which she wove them. It was a splendid, solid affair, perhaps handed down through three or four generations.

'House, house,' she said, indicating her desire to show us her kitchen. It was spotlessly clean with some brightly coloured plates of local manufacture hanging on the walls and – rather incongruously – a huge and very modern refrigerator.

Tia's warmth of heart was too great to be conveyed in her few words of English and so, as we departed, she embraced each of us, talking volubly in Greek. I thanked her in English and told her: 'We shall always remember you, and every time my husband sits with his feet on your mat he will think of you.' She possibly did not understand the words and she certainly did not understand why the rest of the family laughed so much. Our souvenir of Tia is now in situ and gives much pleasure to all who see it.

WATER UNDER THE BRIDGE

I N THE DUSK of a winter afternoon I stood on the bridge and looked down at the river as it flowed on its way towards Wigtown Bay. Earlier in the day the woods on the hillside above me had echoed to the shouts of beaters, the blast of whistles, the sharp tapping of sticks against trees, the cries of 'mark' and 'over,' the sharp report of guns. One after another the rocketing pheasants had fallen, crumpled, leaving, sometimes, a little cloud of feathers floating in the air above them. Now all was over; the beaters and guns had gone home to tea, the dogs to their kennels; silence had descended on the woods.

It was such a silence as seems often to lie about the woods in the days before Christmas – a stillness, a hush, a sense of expectation, almost as though the natural world were conscious of the great festival for which we wait.

Nature, in awe to Him
Had dofft her gaudy trim.

Along the river bank the trees were quite bare except for an ash on which hung still a few rusty-looking bunches of keys. Above the bridge was a deep pool where the water was smooth and peaty brown, hardly seeming to move – a place where salmon lie. Below the bridge it was shallow, running murmurously over the stones, flowing back upon itself here and there to make a white patch of foam.

I shut my eyes and listened to the sound – the enchanting, soothing, evocative sound of running water. It speaks of time, for the river flows as the sand flows through the hourglass, and this water that passes me now on its way to the sea will be gone for ever just as will these moments in which I stand dreaming here on the bridge. Yet, like the hills to which the psalmist lifted up his eyes, the river comforts us with its promise of permanence, for though today's river flows under the bridge and is gone tomorrow's river will take its place and 'as long as the earth remaineth' it will endure.

The plump, black Galloway cattle in the field by the road moved over the brown grass, pulling a mouthful here and there; a solitary gull passed overhead, its outspread wings making a curve against the darkening sky like the curve of the young sickle moon. I thought of this river in the long ago and of those who had watched and listened beside it as I was doing now: Bobby Burns, perhaps, for he knew this countryside well, and it was only a couple of miles from here that he wrote *Scots wha hae' wi' Wallace bled*; Wallace himself, it may be, and young Lochinvar, for legend has it that when he had snatched his bride from Netherby Hall it was to Rusko Castle, just over the trees here, that he brought her. He would have crossed this river often and the young lovers would have walked by it and perhaps fed upon salmon taken from this very pool.

Yet, somehow, when one thinks of Scottish history, it is most often of tragedy that one thinks – of lost causes, of gallant deaths, of bitter battles for a deeply held faith. It is thus with Ireland, too, but with more cause, for all the history of Ireland is sad while all that of Scotland is not. But there is perhaps something in the Gaelic character that produces its finest hours when it faces defeat.

In the long history of Galloway, it is most of all of her martyrs that one thinks. This was Covenanters' country, and their brave, tragic story is written across this landscape in the graveyards and on the hillsides. Stevenson thought of them when he lay, sick for home, in far-off Samoa, writing, writing always despite his mortal illness, and dreaming of the hills

> *Where about the graves of the martyrs the whaups are crying,*
> *My heart remembers how.*

Just over the skyline, four or five miles from here, is Kirkconnell Moor where five men were slain and where a memorial to them now stands. Covenanters on the way to their conventicles, the forbidden services held in secret places on the moors, must have crossed this river and perhaps, somewhere away upstream, the sound of their prayers mingled with the sound of the waters that would flow past this spot.

I left the bridge and wandered along the river bank, and as I looked into the trees I saw suddenly the flick of a white tail, and the shadowy form of a roe deer moved noiselessly into the undergrowth. My thoughts turned abruptly from the far to the near past, from Covenanting history to the happy days of last summer.

I remembered how an eight-year-old girl had prayed to see a deer and how magnificently her prayer had been answered by the sight of a handsome buck drinking at the river half a mile above the bridge on a still, September evening. I remembered a day of hot sunshine when I had sat in the heather beside a burn that flows into this river far upstream and heard the grouse calling 'go back, go back' and watched the line of guns stretched across the moor. I remembered the flushed happy face of the youngest beater and the scene at lunchtime when he and his sister sat beside the keeper, drinking in stories of other days and other shoots, looking like a reconstruction in another setting of Millais' picture where the old sailor tells stories of the sea to two spellbound children. And I remembered cool evenings here by the river – which was then, after the hot summer, almost dry – when the children played boats with twigs under the bridge and gazed into the pool in the hope of seeing a salmon.

When I returned to the bridge it was almost dark and a star had appeared in the sky. Far away an owl hooted. All else was still.

> *Only the mightier movement sounds and passes;*
> *Only winds and rivers,*
> *Life and death.*

HAIL AND FAREWELL

I N THE BRIGHT SUNSHINE of an early March afternoon I heard the chuckle and chatter of a multitude of fleldfares. There was nothing remarkable about that: it was the location that made the sound significant, for it came from a group of tall willow trees in the little valley below the house, and I have never known fieldfares to collect there except when they are preparing for departure.

Through my glasses I watched them, as thick on the branches as dead leaves before the winds of autumn have begun to blow. They all faced one way, and, except for an occasional movement here and there, the flutter of a wing, the flash of a white underside, they sat quite still; yet the stillness did not for a moment conceal the excitement that pulsed through the flock, and I sensed it as one can sense the mood of a crowd, something that is more than just the sum of individual and similar desires. At any moment the birds would erupt, like a bursting firework, upwards into the spring sky, and the whole flock would turn, as one, for the north, travelling high and fast, with strong, purposeful wingbeats, and the willows would be left bare and deserted, and the sound of twittering and chattering would grow faint and die on the still air.

Even though their going proclaims the spring, I cannot see it without a slight and passing sadness. The season that is slipping away reminds one of the unalterable laws of time and mutability, and by that, if by no other means, earns a backward glance of fondness and farewell. Even a winter such as this, with its fogs and frosts and icy winds, has had its moments of beauty, and it will not come again. But no such thoughts troubled the rooks that, in the ash trees just above the fieldfare-laden willows, were busy at their nests. All along the ragged line of desirable residences they were juggling with their furnishings, twisting and turning, re-arranging, squabbling, flying to and fro. Fresh bits of stick arrived every few minutes, and the activity of the builders was viewed with apparent contempt by the idlers who sat among the neighbouring branches and stared. For all the notice any of them took of the chattering fieldfares, the flock might as well have been in Scandinavia already.

I went down the hill and turned right-handed, following the little stream and passing the pond where mallard sometimes breed and moorhens call and splash in the spring nights. Along the banks there were primrose leaves in plenty, but as yet no sign of flowers. I watched two pairs of bullfinches happily picking the buds off a prunus tree, the glossy black heads and brick-red breasts of the males making splendid blobs of colour in the branches. It was a pity to think of the pale, star-like flowers furled within those buds and destined never to open, but nature is prodigal of her splendours and doubtless the prunus blossom will not be visibly diminished by this innocent theft.

The pigeons were crooning their tender, throaty song – 'Tak' two coos, Taffy, tak' two coos, Taffy, tak'.' It is associated in my mind with childhood and the long shadows of summer evenings, and I would defend these musicians, if I could, sentimentally and illogically, against the practical people who destroy them in order to save for our use what the Prayer Book calls the kindly fruits of the earth. I leaned on the wooden bridge to look and listen. Twenty yards below me, a bend in the bank hid the stream from my view, but I could still watch its progress by the rippling shadow that the water threw on to the surface of a stone. By shadows, too, I knew the movements of a party of jackdaws that passed once or twice above my head, and there was a curious, subtle pleasure in seeing the world thus, by reflection – like the Lady of Shalott.

I fell into a reverie. The warmth of the sun, the unhurried murmur of the water, lulled my senses; even the shouts of the children, playing in the road that had suddenly become dry and dusty, sounded from afar as drowsy as the droning of a bee, And, like the bees, who were even now buzzing about the golden cups of the crocuses up on the lawn, the children had felt the spring. Their winter shouts were different – sharper, briefer, carried on smoky breath in the cold air; to-day they let their voices ring and linger, they shouted for the fun of it, because the spring was driving the blood through their veins as the sap is driven through the branches.

A tree-creeper alighted low on the trunk of an ash tree close to where I stood, and began to ascend with hurried, jerky movements, turning its head to right and left, so that its long beak, like a fine, curved needle, could more easily probe the fissures of the bark. Above in the branches, among the ash-keys that still hung, dry and papery, a goldcrest hovered and fluttered in pursuit of insects, moving so rapidly and with so little pause that one could scarcely see the streak of flame on its tiny head from which it has its name. I remembered the nest I had watched being built in a macrocarpa tree last spring – perhaps by this very bird. And soon the labour would begin again, because the spring was here. I found myself listening for the chiff-chaff; no, it was absurd, impossible – the chiff-chaff had never come as early as this. But no amount of cold logic could kill that delicious sense of expectancy.

Turning for home, I heard again the familiar chatter, and looked up to see the whole huge flock of fieldfares passing overhead. Winter had gone. And suddenly and unromantically I was reminded of a railway station where nobody is very interested in the departing train because the signals are down on the other line and everyone is waiting on the arrival platform to welcome the expected travellers.

THE MOLE TRAPPER

I T BEGAN WITH A CRY of anguish early one morning. The master of the house, who had spent the previous afternoon mowing the lawn and had gone to bed very satisfied with its immaculate condition, looked out of the bathroom window to see, strung across its smooth, green surface, a chain of mole-hills. There was despair; there were predictions that the rest of the lawn would soon be similarly disfigured, and the master departed for work exhorting me to do something about it. I went into the town and bought a mole-trap, opened up one of the scars on the lawn and set the trap in the tunnel. I had not much expectation of success, remembering what I had been told about the wiliness of moles and the skill required to catch them. I left the trap in place for two days; nothing happened, but there were no further mole-heaps on the lawn. The scars were trodden down, the sense of crisis passed, and I removed the trap and hung it in the potting-shed.

We continued to be aware of the presence of the moles, but they kept off the lawn. Sometimes when I put a trowel into the border it sank unexpectedly and there was a mole's tunnel; sometimes I saw traces of them in the vegetable garden. But these were harmless places and there was no mess, so we were content to leave the moles in peace.

Weeks passed. Then, one morning, there was another series of earthworks on the lawn, and, plainly, something had to be done.

I remembered that someone had mentioned a mole-catcher in a neighbouring village, and I telephoned to ask about him Apparently Sam was the man I wanted and determined to lose no time, I went straight off to look for him. He was an elderly, round-faced man, lame from an arthritic hip, with a slow, quiet voice and manner. He agreed to come on Saturday afternoon.

At the appointed time I went to fetch him, accompanied by Michael, aged four, who was fascinated but slightly anxious to see what 'the mole man' would look like. Sam emerged from his house looking rosy and benevolent and a friendship was quickly established. He carried a sack, a trowel and some traps.

When we arrived in our garden, I led Sam at once to the earthworks on the lawn, but, to my surprise, he took no interest in them. 'That's just where they've been rooting about,' he said. 'It's not a bit of good putting traps in there.

You have to find their main runs.' With that, he stumped off and began a tour of investigation, followed, at a respectful distance, by Michael and me. At intervals Sam stopped, threw down his sack, and, with difficulty, dropped on his knees. Then he opened up a tunnel with his trowel, nodded, heaved himself to his feet again and went on.

When he had finished his tour, he announced where the traps were to go. He explained that moles must always go to water and that he had therefore looked to see the route by which they would be most likely to travel between their earthworks on the lawn and the stream at the bottom of the hill. I watched him set the first trap. Having opened up the run, he carefully removed with his hand any loose earth from its floor and set the trap in. Then he pulled some handfuls of long grass, rolled them into two fat twists, and laid them across the top of the trap to cover in the run again.

I went indoors and left Sam and Michael to finish the job. From the window I saw them journeying about the garden together, Michael eagerly asking questions, Sam explaining. The mole-trapper departed, instructing me to let him know the results.

That night I had a lot of questions to answer. Why does the mole go into the trap? How does he get caught? Why did the man want to catch him? I was not at ease in my answers, nor even in my conscience. I thought of *The Wind in the Willows*, and of that first bit where Mole is doing his spring-cleaning. And then I feared that, if the moles were caught, it would be anguish for a four-year-old heart. I explained that they spoiled the garden and so they had to be caught in the trap. Four-years-old considered a moment and then said, gravely, 'If I was a mole I wouldn't like it.'

I remembered with a pang that, two days before, I had countered his suggestion that he should tread on a worm by saying, 'How would you like it if somebody very big came and trod on you?' Now I regretted this lesson in identifying oneself with the victim. But untroubled sleep came to the little head on the pillow, and next morning I was invited with great urgency to come and look at the mole traps. We went. I pulled up the first trap. The little sleek, furry body was held tight between the prongs. The curiously appealing nakedness of the tiny paws, so like human hands, smote my heart. But Michael looked at it with detachment, with scientific curiosity, and merely asked why he hadn't got any eyes. I was relieved.

It was a wet day when Sam came again to reset the traps, two more moles having been caught meanwhile. Michael went with him in his yellow macintosh. From the window I saw them bending over one of the traps, together with old George, who was on his way to do some hoeing. Sam took out the body of a mole, showed it to Michael and then tossed it over the hedge. The two men talked. The little boy watched and listened. Suddenly I knew that it was right that the child should imbibe the earthy wisdom of these old countrymen, unsentimental, tender and tough.

Sam's influence was not confined to Michael. For I, after watching his methods, set a trap in the mole-run below the drawing-room window and caught two in three days. Perhaps I have a future in the profession.

THE KINGDOM BY THE SEA

HERE WAS NO languorous heat or scorching sunshine on that beach between the Welsh hills and Cardigan Bay, and if there had been it might have seemed a little out of place, for the Englishness of those summer days was perfectly matched to the scene. The pale blue skies and the white clouds had the same washed purity as the pale blue sea, the wide sands and the smooth, bleached pebbles along the shore. There were no strong colours to assail the eye, no sounds but the rhythmic surge of the sea, the voices of children playing and the occasional cry of a gull.

The children were digging, small bodies bent to their work, heads now and again coming close together in conference over their project; and I thought suddenly of those curiously magical lines from Annabel Lee:

I was a child and she was a child,
In this kingdom by the sea.

Children are the proper inhabitants of the seashore, for they alone can truly appreciate the vastness of the ocean and the minuteness of the delicate treasures that it yields up. Those who lie on the beaches of Europe diligently acquiring the status-symbol sun-tan, the water-skiers, the sophisticates displaying the latest fashions in beach-wear, are not much impressed by the mysterious immensity of the sea since they have probably flown over it in next to no time by jet plane. But to the child it is at once thrilling and awe-inspiring. 'What *makes* the tides?' Michael had asked that morning. 'Is Ireland on the other side of this sea? When the tide is in here, is it out in Ireland?' Alas, I am not good at answering questions directed towards scientific knowledge, since I have none. I could only reply that the rhythm of the tides is linked to the rhythm of the moon and is something that we cannot fully understand.

But if I fail in scientific answers I will yield place to none as a builder of castles. The sand lately washed by the tide was of perfect consistency for the job and, while we worked at the construction of turrets and ramparts, five-year-old Mary ran to and fro with her bucket bringing pebbles to make windows and doors. Each one had to be examined and marvelled at – this one was white as snow, this one grey with a band of pink around it, this one brown and smooth like a potato. All were put into place and became for us at once,

> ... *magic casements, opening on the foam*
> *Of perilous seas, in faery lands forlorn.*

Then we could begin, with our imagination, to people our castle. Since we live, at present, in an atmosphere heavy with history – an atmosphere engendered by the enthusiasm of seven-year-old Michael – it was not at all difficult, and the barriers raised by a sense of time (not yet acquired) were non-existent. Thus we could see King Arthur walking along these ramparts with Queen Guinevere beside him, while from a window the sad prisoner Charles I looked out. On the main tower the flag flew to celebrate the victory of Henry V at Agincourt and across the bridge that we had made so carefully we saw Sir Walter Raleigh departing to join his ship.

Our musings were interrupted by the arrival of Mary with a shell that she had found. It lay on the small, square palm of her hand as she held it for our inspection, smooth, pale grey with horizontal lines delicately traced upon it. We lifted with great care the hinged upper flap to see the empty interior where some tiny sea creature had lain. 'But what has happened to him?' she asked anxiously, 'Has he been eaten?' Probably – but we used the shell for one more decoration on our castle before we went home for lunch. As we departed from the beach, Michael turned back to look again at our creation. The spell broken, he saw it suddenly with the eyes of disenchantment. 'We haven't got those turrets quite right,' he said.

That evening, I stood in the twilight on the hill above the sea, listening to the call of a curlew and, behind it, the unending suck and thump and murmur of the sea. I looked down across the shore and, where our castle had stood, there was now only the smooth and gleaming sand for the tide had come and gone again. In its passage it had erased all the imperfections of our efforts, washed them away to lose them in its own huge, compassionate bosom. Only, I reflected, in our childhood in that enchanted kingdom by the sea can we have thus, every day, a wholly new beginning.

THE MAGIC SPADE

CERTAIN PLACES loved in childhood remain clearly in the memory, every detail easily recalled at will. Such a place for me was the home of my grandparents in Worcestershire. On the last lap of what seemed in those days an inordinately long car journey, one turned off the main road and went uphill past Pex Wood where, in spring, the ground was a blue haze of bluebells flowering under the trees. One then drove through the gate and up a winding drive along the side of a field called Conigre.

There were many delights on my visits there: the doll's house that had been my mother's, the bedroom that had a window seat, the hothouse where grapes were grown and the ginger beer that was made in the house and which we were allowed to drink on special occasions when we had lunch in the dining room. But the most special joy was Conigre. On the far side of this field was the rabbit warren from which it derived its name.

Before myxomatosis almost wiped out the rabbit population, a warren would hold several hundred rabbits in a complicated network of communicating burrows. The soil in Conigre was very sandy, and in the process of digging their underground settlement, the rabbits had deposited a great deal of sand on the surface. Here my brother and I used to dig, making castles and turrets as though we were at the seaside.

My brother, being five years older than I, was allowed to use an iron spade which made it easier to carve out exactly the figure one wanted; I had to make do with a wooden one because it was safer. Halfway across Conigre, we had to pass a hollow tree where Bill kept his spade. He told me (not to tease me but to make my wooden-spade apprenticeship more tolerable) that fairies lived in the hollow tree and gave him the spade, but it was no good asking for one before the age of seven. I accepted this without question and would watch admiringly as he called into the tree, 'Can I have my spade, please?' put in his arm and pulled it out.

I longed and longed to be seven and lay in bed at night thinking about the time when I, too, would be able to put in my hand and receive an iron spade. But the day never came, for when I was six, my grandparents died within a few months of each other, the house was sold and we never went there again.

I often thought of Conigre and wondered if the hollow tree still stood and if Bill's spade was still inside. Once, many years later, I found myself not far from there and decided to go and look. But as I turned off the main road, up the familiar hill where Pex Wood had been, I saw a hideous house with huge plate glass windows surrounded by green tiles, and, beyond it another, and yet another, all of equal ugliness and vulgarity. Birmingham had reached out and gathered Pex Wood and the surrounding fields into its great maw. If it had come this far, perhaps the house that I had loved was gone. And what of Conigre?

I could not bear to see that landscape changed and especially to see our field, our hollow tree, our digging ground, transformed into suburbia. So I turned the car and drove away, keeping the picture of the Conigre of long ago clearly in my memory.

ELEGY FOR A WOODCOCK

W HEELS ON THE GRAVEL, opening and shutting of doors, and voices in the outer hall proclaimed the return of the men of the family from a day's pheasant shooting. Going to greet them, I saw on the floor, among the gun-cases, cartridge bags, dirty boots and wet jackets, two brace of pheasants and a woodcock. This is not an area where woodcock breed, but they come into the woods in winter and so are not infrequently to be found among the bag; yet they are uncommon enough to be regarded as something rather special. I hung the birds in the cold larder, and there they remained for a week to mature.

When pheasants are ready, they are taken to the poultry-monger to be plucked and drawn. Once, as a rather new housewife, I took on, with a jauntiness that was rasher than I knew, the preparation of a pheasant for the pot. It was a day never to be forgotten. I had watched the process so many times without paying much attention to it, talking to my old friend while her hands moved swiftly to and fro over the pheasant's body. It had looked so easy. I did not doubt that I could do it with equal ease, though perhaps not with the speed that comes only from practice.

So I started, and in a few minutes there were feathers everywhere – all over the kitchen, in my hair, up my nose, down my throat – and still, it seemed, just as many on the pheasant's corpse. Somebody, I remembered, had once told me that they plucked birds under water. Perhaps I should try this. So into a bucket of water went the bird, and I renewed my efforts. It was worse – far worse. Wet feathers clung to my fingers and floated in the bucket so that I could not see what I was doing, and when after several hours the plucking was finished there remained the grisly business of removing the bird's insides. Over that a veil shall be drawn. Suffice it to say that I determined never again to undertake this task unless it was all that could save me from starvation.

So when these latest pheasants had hung for long enough, there was no question of their not going to the poultry-monger. But the woodcock was different. The fact that its insides could be left in situ was a great help, and the feathered area was so small that surely even I could deal with it without any great difficulty.

I spread out a good supply of old newspapers on the kitchen table, brought the woodcock, and sat down. I looked at it for a while. It is a bird of great beauty, even in death: the upper parts patterned with buff, black and brown, the wings bearing buff stripes on black, the breast – so soft to the touch – marked with tiny, dark brown bars on the pale background. I remembered most vividly a spring evening in Kerry when we had stood in a woodland clearing within sound of the sea and had watched, in the twilight, the flight of roding woodcock. As each bird came over us in a curious, rapid, rather batlike flight, their wings making no sound, we had heard their strange call, something between a grunt and a snore.

I began to pluck the bird, and the feathers came away easily, but they were so beautiful. that I could hardly bear to see the growing heap of them on the table, each one more delicate and intricate in its pattern than anything that the hand of man could fashion. How mysterious is the world of nature, and how many secrets it still holds, despite the probing of science! Where, I wondered, was this bird reared, and by what route had it travelled to a Wiltshire wood?

Plucking away mechanically, I grieved that so beautiful a creature had to die, and began to compose in my mind an elegy for a dead woodcock. Suddenly, the ridiculous thought struck me that only a horrible misquotation was needed to turn Byron's poem into just that: 'So, we'll go no more a-roding | So late into the night'. 'Not funny,' I told myself, 'and certainly not clever.' But it had cheered me up. Somebody opened the kitchen door and Linnet, the Labrador, excited by the smell of game, rushed in and stood beside me, wagging her tail. The draught that she created sent the small, downy feathers flying into the air and obliged me to spread another newspaper hurriedly over the top of the heap until I made her sit still.

At last the woodcock, bereft of all its feathers, lay on the table before me, a sad, small object. Its head should be turned, Mrs Beeton says, so that the long, straight beak can be tucked under one wing It was not Byron that came to my mind this time, but the nursery rhyme about the robin in the snow: 'He'll sit in the barn, and keep himself warm | And hide his head under his wing, poor thing.'

THE SOUND OF BIRDS

T IS CURIOUS to how many people – country dwellers, too – the voices of birds remain, all their lives, an unidentified background noise, only rarely noticed and never considered worthy of investigation. 'How beautifully', they may say, on a warm spring day, seated in their garden chairs, 'how beautifully the birds are singing today'. But it never occurs to them to wonder which birds are singing nor to look whence the song is coming. I know, because for nineteen years of my life I was like that too. I knew only those voices that one cannot help knowing – the voice of spring which Edward Thomas so beautifully described: 'The cuckoo crying over the utouched dew'. And

the pigeons crooning on summer evenings in the little wood
beside the garden of my childhood; the jay screeching in
alarm, the owl calling in the quiet night. All else was to me,
not a mystery, for that implies something that one would
like to solve, but a closed book which I had no desire to
open. Indeed, I remember being told of a guest who came
sometimes to our house, that she knew the songs of all the
birds and I thought of it as a rather eccentric
accomplishment.

My conversion – for I can only call it that – occurred
quite suddenly one day in a sort of blinding flash. I was
walking through the garden with a young visitor, a boy
whom I knew to be a dedicated ornithologist and, just to
make conversation, I pointed to a little brownish bird on the
tree we were passing and asked idly, 'What is that?' He
answered, 'It's a chiff-chaff, one of the first migrants to
arrive here in spring. Wait a minute and you will hear it'.
Immediately its voice was heard, like a little golden bell of
unimaginable sweetness swinging to and fro in the wind. In
that moment a new world was opened to me, a world in
which I have ever since found unending interest and
enormous joy. I began, for the first time, to look and listen; I
plied my visitor with questions.

I had extraordinary good fortune that spring and
summer. I ought to have been at work in London, listening
not to the song of birds but to the sinister throb of V1s
passing overhead and the even more sinister silence when
the engine stopped. Instead, an attack of jaundice laid me
low and I was sent home to recuperate. It was then late

May, and in the wood and the wild garden (grown wild thanks to Hitler) the willow warblers, the blackcaps, the thrushes and blackbirds and all the rest of the bird population were pouring out a torrent of song.

I was in thrall to this new delight. Hour after hour I stood, sat, crawled, with my binoculars, following a voice until its owner was visible, watching, listening, learning. I was astonished to find how easy it is to learn once you begin to listen. Soon I knew all the commoner voices in the garden. There were moments of particular excitement. The blackcap, who hides so well, eluded me for some time, flying from the middle of one bush to the middle of another, tormenting me with the beautiful song which I could not identify and taunting me with its alarm note, like two stones being knocked against each other. It was a triumph when at last I saw the singer and discovered what it was, Then, of course, there were the nightingales. Not, for me, the most beautiful song but the most celebrated among the poets. That spring, obsessed with this new joy, I used to bicycle in the evenings to a neighbouring wood since there were no nightingales in our own; and while, often the aircraft flew high overhead on their way to carry out a bombing mission, I listened to the rich, tender voices and thought of Bridges's poem: 'Beautiful must be the mountains whence ye come'; and of Keats: 'Thou was not born for death, immortal bird, | No hungry generations tread thee down.'

What is the song of songs, the truly sweetest, greatest? It is impossible to decide. The mood changes, the setting is right or wrong. Just as one day it is a Beethoven symphony that one wants to hear and on another day it is a Chopin étude, so there are times when the blackbird's joyous, jaunty melody seems supreme and others when the tender, sweetly falling song of the willow-warbler touches the heart more deeply. On a still autumn day the robin's song has a poignant beauty, and in the heat of summer the gentle private twittering of swallows is a soothing and delightful sound. Of a quite different kind are the voices of shore and estuary – wilder and more magical. The curlew's call is surely one of the best sounds in Nature, and the clamour of a great flock of wild geese flying overhead is something never to be forgotten. These, for those of us who live inland, are occasional treats. The birds of field and woodland and garden are our more constant companions and their voices, woven into the passing years, carry on from season to season memories of other days and other places.

BIRDS SEEN AND UNSEEN

T HE FIRST TIME I experienced the frustration of failing to see an unusual bird was when, at the age of eight, I was taken by an indulgent uncle on a boat on the Severn from Upton to Tewkesbury. There was a party of us, and someone called out: 'Look, there's a kingfisher!' I was the only one not to respond appropriately with an exclamation of admiration for its beauty. I looked in the wrong place, saying desperately, 'Where, where? Please show me!' The colourful streak stayed for no explanation. Although I was not then particularly interested in birds, I suffered the same disappointment as if I had failed to see a rainbow or missed the view of the White Horse when travelling in the train to London.

Some years later, having become a keen ornithologist, I was to suffer the acute disappointment of arriving five minutes too late at the spot on the Norfolk marshes where a bittern had just been sighted. I have still not seen one.

What an excitement it is to see rarities! They are splendid bonuses on journeys not undertaken with ornithological intent, and I shall always remember the pair of storks that I saw nesting on a chimney in Avila, and the flock of them flying over Jerusalem on spring migration down to the Jordan Valley, the black woodpecker in Berlin, the roller sitting on a telephone wire near Lydda and the little egret flying over a beach in Rhodes.

Dreams of visits to the Camargue or the Coto de Doñana have never materialised. Mention of such an idea once drew genuine surprise from Muthu, our Indian friend and pillar of the household. 'Why go Spain see birds?' he enquired. 'Plenty birds our garden.' Indeed, our garden has produced some rarities. There was a day in late June when I noticed much activity in a pair of poplar trees from which the leaves, apparently plucked off, were floating down in some numbers. When I trained my binoculars on them, I saw two pairs of crossbills.

I had never seen them before except in illustrations, but there could be no mistaking them. The curiously crossed bill, almost like a deformity, identified them at once. The two males were a splendid brick red with dark wings and tails, the females olive-coloured. Why they were pulling off poplar leaves, I do not know. Conifers are their normal habitat. They stayed there all day, and the next morning had gone.

That same summer produced a 'near miss', for, one evening a few days after the crossbills, I heard a quail calling from a cornfield. It kept up its rather pathetic trisyllabic cry, which has been likened to 'Wet-my-feet, wet-my-feet', as long as I was distant, but when I reached the cornfield it fell silent. I stalked it daily for the best part of a week, but had to admit defeat, and I have still never seen a quail.

One morning in early May, three years ago, we had our most spectacular sighting on home ground. I was looking absent-mindedly out of the study window, while telephoning, and saw, at some distance away across the lawn, a bird to which, at first, I paid no particular attention. Then, with part of my mind, I became conscious of something unusual about its shape and movements and, having put down the telephone, I fetched my binoculars. I could hardly believe my eyes. It was a hoopoe.

My husband, writing at his desk, heard my exclamation and enquired the cause. I gave him the binoculars, and he saw this bird, which had been a familiar sight on summer days in the garden of his home in Poland. It was feeding voraciously, pausing now and then to lift its head so that its magnificent crest, although not raised, was clearly visible; so, too, through the binoculars, were its pinkish plumage, black and white bars on wings and tail, and long, curved beak, with which it probed the ground for food.

I grabbed the telephone and rang a friend, a knowledgeable ornithologist. 'You won't believe me,' I said, 'but there's a hoopoe feeding on the lawn.' There was a moment's silence. 'A what?' 'A hoopoe.' 'Good Lord,' he said. 'Can I come and see it?' I begged him to come as quickly as possible, and stayed by the window in an agony of fear that it would depart before he could get here. But all was well. In fifteen minutes flat, he arrived, saw it and photographed it from the window, and it was duly recorded in the notes of the Wiltshire Natural History Society. About lunchtime, it flew off, and presumably continued on the journey that it had interrupted for the meal on our lawn.

There are always some sightings that one cannot be sure about; the worst are when driving. Once, a bird looking rather like a small partridge got up off the road and flew high over the hedge, with its legs dangling, and down into a cornfield. By the time I had stopped the car in an unobstructive position and got out to investigate, there was no sign of it. I think it was a corncrake, but I shall never know. My driving tends, annually, to become a bit erratic around mid-April when something in flight appears to right or left or high overhead and I do want to have a good look at it to see if it is the summer's first swallow.

IN SEARCH OF NIGHTINGALES

THERE ARE SCARCELY ever nightingales within the bounds of our own parish. There was a time when they bred here, and then it was at that period when their singing blended strangely with the roar of bombers passing overhead on their way out to their night's work. The wooded valley would seem perfect for them, but it does not please them, so we must go elsewhere to hear their song.

Three or four miles away there is a big wood which is divided into quarters by the rides that run straight through it in the shape of a cross. In one quarter are the remains of a Roman villa which was discovered eighty years ago when a sporting parson was making an earth for foxes to breed in.

In another quarter is a pool, overhung with trees, called the Black Pond, where once a seaman was robbed and murdered by one of his shipmates. For me it is a special place, not because of these things, but because I walked or rode here almost daily as a child, and it has the enchantment of the places of childhood which nothing can destroy and nothing quite rival. It was here that I went in search of nightingales on a perfect summer evening at the end of a day of warmth and sunshine.

It was twilight already as I drove along the lanes, and the cow parsley foaming between hedge and roadway appeared as two long white clouds stretching out before me, like the feathery vapour trails that I had seen that day stretching across the blue sky in the wake of aeroplanes. There was a light in the woodman's cottage, but the big gates there were shut, and I went on to the far corner of the wood and stopped the car at the roadside. When I turned off the engine, the silence seemed to be absolute, and I shut the door behind me quietly with the feeling that one has in church that it is irreverent to make a noise. The moon was up, more than half-way towards her fullness; I looked up at her through the branches of an ash tree whose leaves were only just opening. 'Come the oak before the ash, we shall only have a splash', the old saying goes, but the ash is nearly always last and all too often opens upon a wet summer. I went through the gate into the field and began to walk along the edge of the wood, and as I went I heard, one by one, the sounds of the night that I had thought silent. Two or three fields away, an owl was calling, 'Kewick,

kewick, kewick'; distantly a, dog barked, and a man
whistled a tuneless tune as he came up the road on his
bicycle. Then a cuckoo began to call, its tender, velvet voice
most beautiful in the dusk. The sky was not quite drained of
light yet; there was still a faint pinkness in the west and
above it a pale, sad green that melted into the blue
overhead, but the evening star was already shining. The
grass was beginning to be wet with dew and the little blue
bird's-eye and the daisies were tightly shut, but I saw an
open white flower at my feet and bent to look at it. It was a
wild strawberry, and I suddenly remembered that they
always grew on the wall at the corner of the wood and that
there had been a particular pleasure in eating them when I
was only just tall enough to reach the plants.

The whistling man had gone out of hearing now, and
the cuckoo was silent, and deep in the wood I could hear
the nightingales. I stood still to listen, and suddenly one
began to sing close by me, in a thicket under some may
trees. One can argue that the nightingale's song is
overrated, that only ornithologists notice it by day, that the
poets have romanticised it and that the blackbird sings just
as beautifully and is made less fuss of. All of which is
partly true. But there is a quality of emotion in this song
that is in no other. To attribute emotion to it is unscientific
and perhaps false, yet I cannot avoid thinking of it in that
way. It is not an effortless song; it has not the gay defiance
of the blackbird's liquid whistle, or the exultation of the
blackcap; it gushes from their throats like blood gushing
from a mortal wound. They seem to be wracked and

tortured by the music that they can neither stay nor fully understand.

'Our song is the voice of desire that haunts our dreams,' Bridges wrote, and he, perhaps more than most of that multitude of poets that have written about the nightingale, has captured the essence of the song. It is desire, one can think if it be not too fanciful, for a world that men have forgotten even to long for until they are reminded by the nightingale. At the heart of all beauty, whether it assails the senses or drives straight into the mind, there is the reminder that we are 'strangers and pilgrims on the earth,' this curious ability to make us feel, as Chesterton so well expressed it, 'homesick though we are at home.'

A faint mist was rising on the fields as the dew fell silently on the warm earth. Sometimes one bird sang, sometimes three or four at once, calling and answering or rivalling one another from different quarters of the wood, and always that throbbing, oft-repeated note fell on the ear like the beating of a pulse, only to die away into the silence of the 'starry woods.' As I stood listening, I thought suddenly of the Roman who had lived here, not two hundred yards from where I stood, and had trod, perhaps this very ground over sixteen hundred years ago. The green things had crept back to the place from which he had banished them, and the earth had closed over all that was left of his house, and the nightingales, caring nothing, sang his requiem.

BIRD-WATCHING BY THE WAY

I HAVE NEVER been on a holiday of which the prime purpose was to watch birds, but wherever I have been the interest of looking at the local bird life has added another dimension to the pleasure of seeing new places.

When I visited that unhappily divided land that was once called Palestine, I knew that I should see some exciting birds, but with all Jerusalem before me, and Bethlehem and Jericho and Hebron, there would not be much time for specifically ornithological expeditions.

My first drive out of Jerusalem was on the winding road to Bethlehem, through a landscape that astonishes –

the brown-ness, the litter of rock and stone everywhere, the bright patches of green corn, the sharp, angular hills, the sudden opening of wide vistas, the flocks of goats or sheep, tended by a herd with a great cloak, looking like people in the Bible illustrations. As we rounded a sharp bend in the road, I saw a vulture soaring easily overhead, floating on massive wings that seemed too big for its body. I saw kestrels that day, too; they are abundant in the country round Jerusalem and are to be seen also in the city. A pair nests every year in the tower of St.George's cathedral and I watched them from the garden in which the Bishop hospitably entertained us; they flew often from the tower into a tall cypress tree, making that curious cry as though they were being attacked.

To the north-west of Jerusalem is a village called Qubeiba which may have been the site of the original Emmaus. Here there is a green valley – green, at least, for that country – full of flowers, for it was spring. I saw wild gladioli growing there, and anchusas and cyclamen; little pied wheatears rose out of the young corn, calling sweetly, and flew in front of us to alight on a stone. Larks sang, and a pair of goldfinches travelled unhurriedly from one clump of thistles to another. Swifts are a part of all that countryside, and in Jerusalem in the cool, blue evening their screaming blends with the cries of children playing before bedtime. In gardens there, I watched greenfinches picking at fir cones, and I saw plenty of the old, familiar sparrows and remembered that five were sold for two farthings but 'not one of them is forgotten before God'.

Seeing the storks was one of the most exciting things. There, people talk of their coming as we talk of the coming of the cuckoo, for they come over Jerusalem in the spring on their way to the Jordan Valley where they breed, and I had been told several times that they would soon be there. I went up to Mount Zion one morning to see the Coenaculum, thought to be the site of the Last Supper, and I emerged from the building in the wake of a party of German tourists to find a fat man gazing up into the sky and crying 'Störchen'. I looked up, too, and there, against the background of brilliant blue, hundreds of huge birds were circling lazily above the city. A few days later, down in the Jordan Valley, where quail breed in the cornfields in great numbers, I saw the storks again and at close quarters. Within sight of the Mount of Temptation, they walked with superb indifference through that terrifying yet beautiful landscape which is like something seen in a nightmare, opening, now and then, their black-edged wings, long necks stretched, legs conspicuously pink.

There was another thrill driving down the road from Jerusalem to the airport. I saw a large bird sitting on the telegraph wire, its head and breast a wonderful, clear, turquoise colour, its back chestnut. It took me a moment to recall the plate in my bird book and to realise that it was a roller, but I had plenty of time to confirm it, for I saw five more along the road.

At the airport I took the plane for Rome and we duly took off, only to be told after 20 minutes that we were turning back because of engine trouble. I had discovered that the girl sitting next to me was the fiancée of the pilot, and when the return was announced she remarked that it gave one great confidence in the safety of the airline as they took no risks. I was not sure that I agreed but thought it better to pretend that I did.

The engine trouble took a long time to put right and so we had to spend an uncomfortable night in the airport hotel. Sleepless, I opened my window in the small hours and heard the creaking call of a corncrake which I had only known before among the lush green fields of County Waterford.

In this bird business it is difficult to decide whether it is more delightful to see something new or to hear a familiar voice calling to you through the dawn or dusk of a strange continent.

DISAPPOINTING COUNTRY

RIVING UP THE NARROW LANE to a remote farmhouse, I saw the large field with a stream running through it and an oak tree standing in the middle. There suddenly came back to me the recollection of a day long ago when I had ridden through that field after hounds.

It was in the last winter before the Second World War, when I was hunting on a very good pony called Silver. I was 15, had just been promoted to 'proper' boots and a stock, and felt almost grown-up. I still enjoyed the pleasurable anonymity of my youthfulness, however, by which I mean that, while my parents' friends and neighbours naturally talked to me, grown-ups not in those categories ignored me.

They tended to be young marrieds – much younger than my parents – who drank pink gins and listened to jazz on their radiograms, or young grown-ups not yet married but flirting a bit with each other. In the hunting field, therefore, I could take the role of a fly on the wall, noting who conversed with whom and often listening shamelessly to the conversation.

On that day, hounds had found a fox and gone away fast over the stone-wall country. I had counted exultantly the walls that I had jumped – thirteen, if I remember rightly. It must be said that stone walls in that area are seldom very big, and all these were of standard size, but I was pleased with what seemed an achievement. Near the stream in this field hounds had checked.

There was a young man who regularly hunted, who was very good-looking and well aware of it. He was tall and fair with a neat, little moustache and long, slender legs that showed off a boot to perfection, and he wore his top hat slightly tilted. He was popular with all the girls and there was usually a little bunch of young people around him. It amused me to observe his social life in the hunting field, and I sometimes deliberately put myself in a position to do so, but on that day it was quite accidental that, when the hounds checked, I found myself on the edge of a small group of which he was the centre.

The horses were sweating after their gallop, and the steam rose from them into the cold air. Our hero – for so he shall be called – was riding a grey horse. He leaned back languidly in the saddle and stretched out his right leg, looking down at the gleaming boot, speckled here and there with mud.

'Awfully disappointing country this is to ride over,' he said. 'You think you have been going damned well for the last half-hour and then you look round and find a child on a pony alongside you.'

So securely was I cocooned in the new-found confidence bestowed by my boots and my stock that for a moment I failed to realise his meaning, and looked round for the 'child on a pony'. But there was none; and then the full import of his remark struck home. He meant me!

Crimson with fury, I turned Silver's head and rode away out of earshot and out of sight of the detestable young man. The humiliation far outweighed the pride of the thirteen walls, and my day was spoiled.

The passing years turned the young man into an old one, who, presumably, ceased to care so much about getting there before everyone else. They turned me into an adult who had no desire to get there at all and was happy to consign the once treasured boots to a jumble sale.

HARRY AND THE CAPTAIN

ARRY WAS THE GROOM who took us out riding
when we were children, first on our small ponies
on a leading rein, then on larger ones in a more
independent manner, and then out hunting at times when
our parents were otherwise occupied. He had started his
working life as a stable boy, then served in the First War in
my father's yeomanry regiment in Egypt and Palestine, and
then returned to look after his stables.

On our rides, Harry used to tell us thrilling and
gruesome stories about the war, of sticking his sword into
Turks and tossing the bodies off the end of it. At some stage
he had lost an eye, but I think that was an accident, not a
war wound, and he never wanted to talk about it. We

children, however, were much interested in the glass substitute and always longed for him to take it out so that we could have a good look at it.

Harry took me hunting one day, when I was about twelve, on my pony called Kitty. She was a good pony but occasionally had fits of obstinacy when she would refuse to jump some perfectly normal little obstacle, and that was what happened on this day. Hounds were running, and we had followed along in the rear very happily for a couple of miles when we came to a wall – quite low – which had to be jumped out of the road into a grass field. Harry jumped it and I tried to follow, but Kitty stopped dead. I took her back and tried again with the same result. After a few more ineffectual efforts, Harry jumped his horse back to my side of the wall and dismounted.

'Come on', he said. 'You hold this one and I'll put her over, the little monkey.'

I stood, holding his horse and Harry got on to Kitty, shook the reins, dug in his heels and told her to get on with it. Kitty gave every appearance of intending to jump until she reached the point of take-off and then dug in her toes. This happened several times and Harry had got very red in the face and had called Kitty some names that I had never heard before, when a car stopped in the road and the Captain got out.

He was a near neighbour, a very tall man, late of a cavalry regiment, full of charm and something of a dandy. He was an official of the Pony Club, to which we belonged but whose rneetings we seldom attended as my father disapproved of it. He said it was snobbish because the farmers' children were not in it. I think that has long since been put right.

The Captain came over and asked if we were having trouble. I explained what had happened and he said perhaps he could help.

'Let me have a go,' he said to Harry. 'I thnk I can deal with her.'

Harry's expression clearly said, 'What makes you think *you* can do it?' but he dismounted and handed Kitty over. The Captain's long and elegant legs were clad in jodhpurs and he was soon astride the errant pony. He turned her round and walked her up the road for some distance, then turned back to where we stood and, with a word of encouragement to Kitty, popped her over the wall. Then he cantered her round in a circle and returned, jumping the wall again. He got down and handed me the reins.

'She's all right now,' he said. 'Just a matter of understanding. I'll wait and see you over.'

I got on and we jumped the wall. I shouted my thanks and he waved and went back to his car. Harry followed me over the wall and we set off across the field. He was silent for some time; then he said: 'I don't like people that's too full of theirselves.' He paused, and then muttered, half to himself, 'I wish she'd 'ave dropped 'im in a cowpat.'

I felt that he was being a little unfair to the captain, but I am bound to say that I, too, found him always 'too full of himself' and the ease with which be had solved the problem that was beyond us *was* very irritating.

One day, a week or two later, I went to the saddle-room and found Harry polishing a curb chain.

'Seen the Captain lately?,' he asked.

'No,' I said. 'Why!'

'The other morning, when I was exercising, 'e was riding that young chestnut of 'is in the big field up by the Fosse, and she bucked 'im off. Bit of a job to catch a 'orse in a field that size.'

'Yes. did you help him?' I asked.

'Oh no,' Harry answered. 'I was just riding along the road, see, and the field was on me left side where me glass eye is, so of course I didn't see nothing,' and he went on polishing.

LIVING FOR THE MOMENT

HE PUPPIES were born on a cold, blustery day in early spring. Linnet, our first yellow labrador, had been restless and unhappy all the night before, and by 7am she was in great distress, panting heavily, rushing into the big box that had been prepared for her and throwing the straw about, then coming out to lie for a few moments on the stone floor, seeking vainly for a comfortable position.

The only previous canine confinement I had attended had been almost effortless, and I had not anticipated such trouble for Linnet. At 7.30 I rang the vet to tell him what was happening. 'Quite normal for the first stage of labour,' he said cheerfully. 'Let us know later if you are worried.'

It was after 11 am when at last the first wet little bundle shot out on to the straw. Linnet was quite calm now and began at once to lick it energetically. It was a yellow girl and, a few minutes later, another followed. My relief was infinite. When Linnet had time to pause from her work of licking, she looked at me and her eyes were already quite different, full of tenderness and pride. Four more puppies were born, and, when all was over I despatched a cable to my husband who was in Hong Kong: 'Six babies born safely. Four black, two yellow.' I thought that might cause a raised eyebrow at the hotel.

Linnet was a wonderful mother, and the puppies thrived. We gave them temporary names, and the paler of the two yellow girls we called Blondie. She was a bewitching little thing – her face was almost white with a darker shade around the nose, which was itself quite black – and we thought she was the one we would keep. She was slightly smaller than the others and, as they grew, the difference in size became more marked. She was also quieter, but she was quite lively and seemed healthy. One day, when they were all playing, Blondie, in high spirits, walked a few paces, gave the best imitation she could manage of a bark and fell over from the effort.

But, a few days after I had started the puppies on cereal, I was with them after their meal, and I saw that while all the others played boisterously, Blondie was sitting in the corner. As I watched, her head drooped like a little dying bird's until her nose almost touched the floor. Something was very wrong.

There followed, during the next two days, three visits to the vet. On the third occasion I had to leave her for an X-ray, and he promised to ring me when I could collect her. His call came five hours later: Blondie had an incurable defect in the stomach which was all right when Linnet was feeding her but which had shown up as soon as she got on to solid food. 'The only thing to do is to put the poor little mite out of pain.'

How, in just over four weeks, had this little creature become so entangled in our affections? And how could one understand this brief life, created but not to endure? Luckily, Linnet, unable to count, noticed nothing, but when the puppies played I could almost see Blondie there with them, and at mealtimes the sixth bowl was like an empty chair.

We were all sad, pretending to cheerfulness, but wise words healed. 'It is the miracle of life that is important, not its duration.' I remembered Blondie's one outburst of high spirits when she barked and fell over. Perhaps it was for that moment that she had lived.

So it was the darker girl who stayed with us, and was called Puffin. In the late summer evenings she and Linnet chased each other across the lawn, in and out under the weeping beech tree which has always featured in the games of the children and the puppies who have grown up here.

THE POACHERS

ATIENCE was a black Labrador, bred at home and later sent to be trained as a gundog. She was of a very gentle nature, extremely obedient, and always did everythinq expected of her except that she failed to produce puppies. The two unions that she had were fruitless probably because of an injection that we had been obliged to get for her earlier, after she had escaped when in season and disappeared into the bushes with a socially and genealogically undesirable male. We therefore imported a yellow Labrador puppy called Linnet, and, as Patience was much too kind to be jealous, the two became firm friends.

It was the friendship that caused them to be guilty of their single fault for it was one that is only fun when committed in company with a friend – hunting. They would sometimes disappear for half a day and return to sit outside the back door, muddy, hungry and ashamed. We were always puzzled at how they managed to depart together and so stealthily that ten minutes after the last sighting of them they had vanished.

One summer day, however, when we had become more watchful, I saw the disappearing act carried out with an art born of practice. We were sitting in the garden and the dogs were with us, Linnet stretched out on her side and Patience lying with her head on her paws. After a while, I sensed rather than saw a sign pass between them. Linnet got up and wandered lazily to the rough grass round the plum trees at the edge of the lawn. She sniffed about with interest as she sometimes found mice there, but it was not mice that she was thinking of. After a few minutes, Patience joined her, also sniffing for mice. They moved slowly towards where the short, rough grass gave way to really long grass like a hayfield, for the old orchard was only cut a couple of times in the year. They were then out of sight.

I got up and walked across to where I could see over the orchard, and there, already halfway across it, were the two dogs trotting rapidly and purposefully in the direction of the farm and whatever pleasures lay beyond it. I had to admire the skill with which they had calculated at what point they would vanish from our view and be able to hurry instead of saunter.

These expeditions did not happen very often, but there came e day in winter when they disappeared and subsequently caused us some embarrassment. They were away all day – much longer than usual – and it was dark when they came home. They were both exhausted and very hungry and shamefaced. They were scolded and put into the literal and metaphorical doghouse.

The next day, my husband had been invited to shoot with some neighbours who have a big wood on their farm. To reach it by road one has to travel about four miles, but if riding or walking one can cross the river by a farm bridge, reducing the journey by half. George, who had retired from working on the farm and then helped us in the garden, went, too, as a beater. He was the son of a keeper and keenly interested in shooting.

When the guns had assembled, their host addressed them. 'I am afraid,' he said, 'we may not find as many birds as usual in the covert. Yesterday, I am told there were two damned dogs running through it, a black one and a yellow one, so they may have messed it up for us completely. I've no idea where they came from; somebody said they thought they belonged to the gypsies that have been around here this week.'

My husband cast a sidelong glance at George who was looking fixedly at his boots. That 'black one and yellow one' was terribly suggestive and their possible owner felt very uncomfortable.

When he came home in the evening – having had a day that was luckily not spoiled by the poachers – we discussed the situation. That covert was right out of the territory known to the dogs and they could not possibly have known where the bridge was. Had they swum across the river? And how could they have known that a covert with pheasants in it lay half-a-mile away on the other side?

My husband considered what to do next. Had the shoot been spoiled by the previous day's trespassers, he would have felt obliged to go and own up and make his humble apologies. But it had not been spoiled and we could not know for certain that they were our dogs. There was always a chance that they *had* come from the gypsies' camp. But, at that point, penitence gave way to indignation.

'Gypsies' dogs!' their master exploded, 'with Field Trial Champions in their pedigrees and their good looks, how could anyone think that they were gypsies' dogs?'

Time has taken Patience and Linnet from us. Perhaps, when they grew old and arthritic, they savoured the memories of their days hunting, and perhaps that one in particular. When I drive, as I often do, along the road from which one can see that covert, I sometimes wonder if the shades of a black dog and a yellow one are ever seen among the trees.

SPOILT STATESMEN

W HEN THE AUNT and Uncle returned from India in the late '20s – the Uncle having retired as a general – they bought a house in Scotland with some shooting and fishing. Dogs were a necessary part of that sort of life, and, since they had no children, their dogs came in for a larger share of the Aunt's affection than would otherwise have been the case. The trouble was that they always had spaniels that were sent to be trained by a local keeper, who knew full well that, no matter how well behaved were the pupils that he sent home to the General, they would soon be spoilt by the General's wife.

It amused the Aunt to call them after statesmen, and the first one I remember was Mussolini. Before the Second

World War, my father took, each year, a grouse-moor in Argyllshire, where birds were walked up in beautiful surroundings for a moderate bag. Of course, the Aunt and Uncle were invited to stay, and arrived accompanied by Mussolini and driven by the chauffeur. Mussolini, a black and white springer, had some disgusting skin disease for which the vet had recommended plunges in salt water. The chauffeur had to take him down to Loch Fyne each evening and submerge him (all but his head). Neither of them enjoyed this proceeding, and the chauffeur was heard to say in colourful language that he would gladly drown the brute.

Mussolini, allegedly trained, was brought up to the moor on the first day. Guns and beaters were marshalled in line, and we set off. When the first covey of grouse got up, the Uncle got a right and left and Mussolini lost his head. Away he galloped, ears flying, oblivious to the Aunt's imploring calls: 'Muss, Muss, come here.'

The line waited, all in some embarrassment. 'When you've got your damned dog under control,' my father shouted, 'we'll get on with the shoot – if there's anything left to shoot at.'

Of course, there was not, and at lunchtime the bag consisted only of the Uncle's brace. The Aunt, having scolded Mussolini in her crossest voice (she was not good at being cross), felt sorry for him and gave him a chocolate biscuit.

Then came the war, so it was some years later that I went to stay with the Aunt for a weekend. Mussolini had by then departed this life, like his namesake, although a good deal more comfortably. Instead, there was General Smuts, who was elderly and bad-tempered, and Oo-Tin-Toot, called after the Burmese secretary general of the United Nations, but answering to a diminutive of Tooty. He was young, amiable and irrepressible. Both dogs occupied chairs in the drawing room, but sometimes, like elderly club members, they both felt they had a right to the same chair.

On Sunday evening, the Aunt turned on the wireless to hear the hymns, and Smuts and Tooty howled in unison throughout, which she enjoyed immensely. That diversion over, they both headed for the best chair by the fire, and Smuts snapped at Tooty. The Aunt aimed a kick at Smuts (which missed) and, grabbing him by the collar, said that he was a naughty boy and would now be shut in the gents' as a punishment. Ten minutes later she relented and let him out, whereupon he jumped on to the sofa with a triumphant glance at Tooty.

The Aunt had bought a farm after the war, from which she derived enormous pleasure but no profit. However, at breakfast on the morning of my departure she opened the post and announced that she had received a cheque for £250 from the Ministry of Agriculture. Shortly afterwards, Tooty was seen galloping out of the front door with a piece of paper in his mouth, pursued by the Aunt calling 'Tooty, Tooty, bring back my cheque, you naughty dog'.

I never heard how the Ministry reacted to the request to send another cheque because the first one had been eaten by the dog.

HIS GREATEST PRIDE

A WELL-KNOWN CHARACTER has gone from the village. While the north-east wind, sharp as a razor-blade, blew over the snow-covered earth and the first lambs were being born, the shepherd relaxed his last, frail finger-hold on life and quietly died.

His name was Ernest, but to most of us he was the shepherd, and it was thus that his wife always referred to him. It signified, on our side, respect for his age and his position in the village, and, on his, a proper pride in his calling – a pride that has been handed down since the days when great flocks of sheep grazed the Cotswolds and men like him were, so to speak, stewards of the great wealth that built the 'wool churches' of Gloucestershire.

The circumference of his life was small; he died about five miles from the place of his birth. His life was spent, until his health failed, in hard work: bitter nights out in the lambing pens, wet days trudging through the mud with a sack over his shoulders to keep out some of the rain.

In his youth and middle years he earned a small wage, and there was no comfort of a hot bath to come home to. But he had always been content. He loved his sheep, as any good shepherd must do, and he gave them his skill and his care ungrudgingly. He never, so far as I know, went away for a holiday.

For recreation he went to the pub in the evenings, where he liked to drink a little and talk a lot. In winter he stopped the foxes' earths when hounds were coming this way, and he liked to feel that he was an important part of the hunt. He did a bit of carpentering, and he used to cut wood from the hedges and make walking sticks of which he was very proud. He was not without a charming and childlike guile. Someone for whom he made one of these sticks told how the offer of payment was met with a firm: 'I don't want nothing for it. You're welcome.' Pause. 'Of course, Mr Jones did give I 10 bob for the one I made for 'e, but I don't want nothing for yours.' The 10 shillings was quietly handed over and as quietly accepted.

The shepherd worked for more than 40 years on the same farm, for which he was awarded a long-service medal by the Royal Agricultural Society. He received a letter, telling him of the award and suggesting that he might like to receive it at a ceremony in the local market. He treated this idea with amused contempt. 'I ain't got no time to go bicycling round the country collecting medals,' he said. 'I be too busy.'

His talk was wholly uncontaminated by the language of radio, television and the popular press. His English was that of his native county, and when he wanted to enrich his speech with a simile he thought of one instead of reaching for the ready-made phrase. When I enquired for the welfare of his leg after a fall, he said the bruise looked 'all like bits o' pickled cabbage'. He transposed pronouns lavishly. When the owner of the farm where he worked sold it and moved away, he told everyone: 'O' course 'er did want I to go wi' she.'

He had one sister who, at the age of 19, had married and gone to live in Canada. He never saw her again, although they always kept in touch. At the time he received his medal, she lay dying, believing herself back in the home of her childhood and wandering, in her talk, about the fields and woods of Wiltshire. The shepherd cut out of the local paper the report of his award, which was accompanied by a photograph of him holding two sheep.

Afterwards, he heard that the cutting had arrived just before she died. ''Er daughter did write to I,' he said, 'as 'ow my letter come that morning. 'Er took it up to our Ethel and 'er said: 'Look, Mum, what I got 'ere.' Our Ethel did look, and 'er were that muddled 'er said, 'It's our Hernest a-holding two helephants.' 'Now, Mum,' 'er daughter says, 'you know there ain't no helephants in Hengland.''

The shepherd would never, I think, have retired. The idea would not have occurred to him, but his working days ended when he was repairing a drystone wall, was seized with pain in his back, and had to be brought home by his son in a wheelbarrow. He enjoyed recounting this drama. He got somewhat better, but was never quite well again and, before long, he took to his bed, where he spent the remaining years of his life. He lay near the window and watched the seasons come and go and talked about the past. He was too far from the sheep to hear the voices of the lambs that entered the world as he prepared to leave it. But, no doubt, he thought about them. With Shakespeare's shepherd he could have said 'the greatest of my pride is to see my ewes graze and my lambs suck'.

DROP O' GINGER WINE

N OUR LITTLE VILLAGE of Norton we have our share of long-lived inhabitants but, as far as I can remember, Our Annie was the only one who managed to reach the century.

Her husband, Ernest, had worked as a shepherd on one farm for more than fifty years. He was a regular visitor to the local pub, where his many anecdotes were often concerned with Our Annie. When he was 88 his back gave out and he could only walk with considerable difficulty. After this he took to his bed, and Annie looked after him for the remaining five years of his life.

She then had 20 years of widowhood. Annie was small of stature and very thin, but, until the day she died, her back was as straight as any soldier's on parade, and it symbolised her natural dignity and pride.

She must have been lovely as a girl, when Ernest courted and married her, for Annie was still good-looking as an old woman. Not a great talker (Ernest talked enough for both of them), she spoke a beautiful, pure Wiltshire dialect. I suppose it was the last I shall ever hear except on a record, for hers was the last generation to be free from the pervasive influence of centralised schooling and BBC English.

When the multitude of daffodils was in flower in the orchard, my mother always picked bunches of them for all the people in our cottages, and I carried on with the practice. When I knocked on Annie's door and she saw the flowers, she would say, 'Oh, they be nice. Be they for I?'

But I found choosing appropriate Christmas presents for Annie extremely difficult. One year, on receiving a scarf, she said: 'I don't never go out to wear 'un'; the following year, her response to a box of sweets was: 'I can't eat they. 'Tis me stomach, see.'

For several years I gave her tea in a decorative tin until she said: 'I don' know why everybody de give I tea.' Desperate, I tried a pot plant, but she eyed it dubiously and said; 'They de always die wi' I.'

When Annie's 90th birthday was approaching, I asked her whether she would be able to drink something for the occasion. 'I shall 'ave a drop o' ginger wine,' she said, 'It de seem to soothe me stomach'. This information was a great help, and thereafter my gifts of stem ginger, crystallised ginger or ginger wine were received without criticism.

When she was 91, Our Annie stood on a chair to dust the top of a picture, overbalanced, fell and broke her pelvis. We all rather thought it would be the end of her, but not at all. She returned from hospital in excellent form and resumed her housework.

As her hundredth birthday drew near, all her neighbours conferred about what to give her. Someone had once heard her say that she would like a rocking chair, so that was what we got, and the youngest inhabitant presented it to her.

Annie began to decline after that. She had one or two 'queer turns' and had to go into hospital where she could be nursed. She was quite contented. 'They be very good to I,' she said, and, indeed, she was a rather special pet of the nurses, most of whom had never met anyone quite like her.

She died peacefully aged 102 and lies buried in the little churchyard, together with Ernest.

ROY AND ADA

W HEN I PASS THE COTTAGE which now has a
white-painted front door, cherry trees in the
garden, modern conveniences inside and garage
outside, I remember how it used to look when Roy and Ada
lived there. It was then virtually unchanged since it was
built in the nineteenth century by the Vicar to house a
sexton. There was no white paint on the front door – or
anywhere else – no running water, sanitation or electricity.
The existence of such discomfort was not then as
uncommon as it is now, and Roy and Ada, having lived
there all their married life, were, at the worst, resigned, at
the best accustomed to it.

Roy, in return for this *un*commodious accommodation,
rang the church bell on Sundays and dug graves when
necessary, attending the funerals in a black suit grown

green with age and a battered bowler hat. In his regular employment he worked for the District Council as a road man. The verb was open to argument, for the job was known by all to attract the laziest characters in every village. The duties were to shovel mud off the road, keep the ditches and drockways clear and cut the grass on the verges in the growing season. The 'length man' as he was called, looked after his own area without supervision, so the job afforded plenty of time for leaning on a shovel and talking to anyone who passed by, or – in summer – for sitting on the verge drinking cold tea and contemplating the landscape. As a matter of fact, the bluish tinge of Roy's nose, which increased as the years went by, suggested that it was not always tea that he carried in his haversack, and he was a pretty regular customer at the pub.

His wife was 'Aunt Ada' to all the village. It was largely a courtesy title, for she was related only to a few. She was a little woman, thin and frail-looking, and her nose, too, had a characteristic of its own though it was not, as in Roy's case, anything to do with the colour. It looked as though it had at some time received a sharp blow on the end which had turned it permanently upward so that her nostrils appeared as two horizontal cavities. She cleaned the church on Fridays, dusting the pews, sweeping the coconut matting and, when all was done, putting the key back in that universally known hiding place, under the doormat.

Ada was less verbose than Roy, but she had an original turn of phrase. Once, after a church council meeting, the members were taken round a garden where primulas grew along the side of a stream. Ada studied them with interest. 'What's them?' someone asked her. 'Well, they'm a sort of educated cowslip,' she replied.

The village is a small one, so it often happens that a year passes with neither baptism nor funeral in the little church. But one year it happened that two members of the community died within a month. Aunt Ada was approaching 80 and had not been well for some time; the sound of Roy's pickaxe in the churchyard seemed ominous to her. 'People de always go in threes,' she said, 'and I shall be the third.'

It was only a few weeks after the second of the two funerals that Aunt Ada, having given Roy his breakfast and seen him off to his length of road, went outside to empty the teapot in the garden. As she went along the flagstone path, she suddenly doubled up and fell, the teapot clattered to the ground and broke, and Aunt Ada was dead. Her premonition that she would be 'the third' had been correct.

That evening, a neighbour went to offer sympathy to Roy. He looked stunned, and all he said was 'It's a bad job'. Thus do the unlettered express their grief. They have no fine words at their command, no healing sentences on their lips, and they have often not even an understanding of the fitness of silence when language cannot be made to obey the heart's command. So they must use for the death of a wife, for a son's birth or a daughter's disgrace, for all the tragic, terrible and beautiful moments of their lives, the words that are as well-worn as their working clothes. A dead cow, a happy marriage, the fall of an empire, may all be met with the same brief sentences, and the whole range of human emotion from supreme joy to devastating sorrow is covered by the two laconic phrases, 'a bad job' or 'a good job'.

Roy followed the sympathising neighbour to the gate and stood there, awkwardly. He took off his cap, scratched his head and replaced the cap, all in one movement of his right hand.

''Twas a pity about the teapot, too,' he said. 'That were 'er mother's and it made a lovely cup 'o tea. The wife'd be upset about that.'

BIDDA

WHEN I PASS the huge refrigerators in the supermarket and see the packets of puff pastry, I think of Bidda's pastry and of how she would have scorned this labour-saving item for which so many people nowadays are thankful. Her puff pastry was a gourmet's dream – jam puffs as light as fantasy, mince pies, vol-au-vent cases. 'Just roll it out every fifteen minutes,' she would say.

'But how do you have *time*, and how do you remember to do it every fifteen minutes?' I would ask.

'Oh, it's quite easy when you're doing other things in the kitchen. It just seems to fit in.'

Bidda was born in Shrewsbury five years before the end of the nineteenth century, and she started her working life as a scullery maid in the great houses of Shropshire. A pale, thin little fourteen-year-old, she went down in the early mornings to clean out, blacklead and relight the kitchen range and then stood at the sink, working her way through seemingly endless stacks of plates, dishes and saucepans. When she had a rare hour of freedom, she ran across the fields to the railway line to see the train going by which could have taken her home.

But she was not unhappy; there was comradeship and laughter among the younger servants, and she never lost sight of her ambition to become a really good cook. She moved a step nearer to that when she became a kitchen-maid, where she was – in both senses – in a position to see more of what went on in the kitchen. Much depended, of course, upon the cook; there was one, of whom she always spoke with great affection, who taught Bidda all she could and gave her opportunities to try her hand. Another, less generous, told her nothing, and sometimes locked herself in the stillroom when she was making something the secret of which she did not wish to share.

It must have been in her years as kitchen-maid (and under the kindly cook) that Bidda learned certain invaluable tricks of deftness. When she made mayonnaise – I see her in my mind – she stood at the table in the scullery (because it was cooler than the kitchen) with the bowl in front of her held steady by the dishcloth that she had rolled up and laid on the table in a circle. She held the bottle of olive oil horizontally, its base pressed against her left hip, its neck held from above by her left hand and her left index finger in the mouth of the bottle so that it controlled the thin stream of oil running down on to the egg-yolks while her whisk rotated evenly and steadily. The sound of a whisk tapping against the side of a bowl is to me inseparable from the thought of Bidda.

In the spring of 1914, she had what seemed a great piece of luck. The position of head kitchen-maid at Attingham Park became vacant; Bidda applied for it, and got it. This was one of the grandest of the Shropshire houses; Lord and Lady Berwick entertained a lot, and the standard of cuisine was well known to be in the first rank. Two or three years in this job would add to her knowledge considerably, and she planned that then she would try for a place where there was a chef to teach her even greater skills. But the 'best-laid plans' of many fell apart in that year of catastrophe; war broke out on the 4th of August and Attingham was turned into a hospital. Bidda spent the next four years cooking for wounded soldiers.

In spite of her disappointment, she made the best of things, hoped that the fulfilment of her plans was only postponed, and put all her efforts into producing the best possible food for the patients. No doubt many a wounded soldier was cheered by eating her apple pie.

But after 1918 the world had changed. There was never again the large-scale entertaining that had been common in many country houses, where dinner-parties were served seven or eight courses, and Bidda's dream of learning the higher flights of cookery from a chef was never to be realised. Her loss, however, was our gain, for after working as a cook in London for a while she came to my parents in Wiltshire, a year before I was born. All through our childhood she made delicious puddings for the nursery, cakes to be sent to my brother at school, beef tea or chicken broth when we were ill, and iced cakes for our birthdays.

The move to us shaped the rest of her life: after fourteen years, she married the chauffeur who had been my father's batman in the First World War. She ceased to be our cook then, and they moved into their own cottage; but two years later, when the Second World War started, she said she would come back into the house and cook for the duration. Kitchen-maids became extinct, and poor Bidda was on her own; it was very different from the future she had once dreamed of, but she accepted it as philosophically as she did all life's vicissitudes. When the war ended she stayed on with my parents, caring for my mother until she died, and only retired, after thirty-two years, because her husband became seriously ill. They went to live in his home village in Worcestershire, where he died, after which she returned to Shrewsbury.

I had married in the meantime and soon afterwards, by extraordinary good luck, we found ourselves living in Shropshire where my husband was doing his last job in the RAF. So we saw Bidda constantly; if we had a lunch or dinner party she came to stay, to cook for it, giving great enjoyment to us and our guests but also to herself, for her passionate interest in her art never diminished.

It is said that to cook well one must be a bit greedy, but Bidda was not interested in eating rich or elaborate dishes. She understood the subtleties of flavour and could read a recipe and imagine how the dish would taste, as a musician can hear the music in his head when he reads a score, but as a meal for her own personal pleasure she would always have chosen roast beef or lamb and a fruit pie.

There were certain dishes she cooked that I have never met anywhere else; her delicious gnocchi, for instance, which were not made with semolina, as they always seem to be in Italy. Instead, Bidda made a thick cheese sauce with eggs in it and poached spoonfuls of the mixture, as one would poach the semolina. Perhaps gnocchi is made like that in some Italian region; stupidly, I never asked her where she learned the dish. Over the years she had collected a thick book of recipes which was, of course, among her greatest treasures. After she retired it was stolen by a cook who was certainly dishonest and probably indifferent, so the book was wasted on her. To the end of her life Bidda always enjoyed reading recipes in the Sunday papers, and when we had been out to a meal would always say, 'May I ask what you had?'

When we moved back to my old home in Wiltshire she stayed with us frequently, and when she began to suffer a degree of disablement from arthritis she came to live with us. The light tap, tap, of her footsteps had always been as swift as the tap of her whisk against the bowl, but now she moved slowly and with the aid of a walking frame. It must have been an agonising frustration for her, but she never complained. She was, indeed, a perfect example of how to grow old. Instead of lamenting her own lost activities, as most of us do in old age, she enjoyed them vicariously through her fervent interest in everything our children did. She had always loved the country, and now that she could no longer walk across the fields as she used to do, she enjoyed sitting in the garden or going with us for a picnic. She soaked up all the beauty of earth and trees and flowers and remembered it afterwards with gratitude for having seen it.

Our children were like dearly-loved grandchildren to her, and she worried that our daughter, growing up, showed no interest in cooking. 'What will she do when she's married?' she used to say. 'She'll have to cook then.' When Bidda died she left each of the children a hundred pounds and as Mary was working in publishing and her thoughts had begun to turn to writing, she bought herself a fine typewriter. The strange thing is that she then began to be interested in cooking, and proceeded not only to practise it but also to write about it, becoming, in due course, the author of cookery books and many articles on the history and origins of various kinds of food.

I do not think the typewriter was a magic one, but I do believe that Bidda in Heaven (for she is most certainly there) asked that Mary might become interested in the subject for which she herself cared so much.

A child, questioning me one day about the next world (in the belief that I knew what it is like!) asked, 'Shall we eat when we get there?' I said, 'No, because we shall have spiritual bodies and we shan't need food.' But since Bidda went there, I have thought again about that answer. The Church teaches us that we shall have in Heaven everything that is needful for our happiness:1 do not think Bidda could be perfectly happy without cooking, and she would need people to eat and enjoy what she cooked to complete her pleasure.

So, should another child ever ask me that same question, I think I should have to answer it differently.

NANNY

TODAY, OCTOBER 22nd, Nanny has gone on her last journey. Like all her journeys, she had prepared for it long before. Just as she always used to be buttoned into her coat, gloved, hatted, sitting in the hall with her stripey canvas bag beside her, so she has been, for some time now, waiting on the threshold, her few treasured possessions bequeathed, her rent carefully paid, her last instructions given. But of this last and longest journey of her life she was not afraid as she had been of all the others. 'Oh' she used to say, when a train had to be caught, 'I feel all sick and worked up'; she used to get very pink in the face and very silent and not want to eat. And one of her most frequent dreams was of travelling with children and missing trains or losing the luggage or – worse still – the children so that she would say in the morning, 'I've been that worried all night'.

This time she had no children to take, and the only luggage she had could not go with her and so was left behind – her bed, her old black handbag, her crucifix, her tattered prayer book, her grey, woollen stockings, her bedroom slippers and her poor old, crooked, worn-out body, sloughed off like a snake-skin. Peacefully, quickly, quietly, without any fuss, she went Home.

Nanny loved giving. She loved the secrecy and surprise in going surreptitiously to the shop and hiding the carefully wrapped parcel until the day of Christmas or birthday came. And all her life was given away with reckless generosity. The days and nights of her youth and of age were given to a sucession of children, and, with perfect contentment, she pushed the perambulators, bathed the little bodies, held the feverish hands, padded through the nursery in her flannel dressing-gown, with her hair in a plait down her back, to take a temperature or comfort a child awake. Her faith and her work were all her life and she never doubted, never questioned, either the one or the other, never wanted any happiness except what these two could give.

Nanny knew all there was to know about babies and children, but of what is commonly called knowledge – of facts and dates and figures – she didn't have much. Yet sometimes she would startle one with that old, old wisdom that is not to be found in books, with a swift summing-up of a person or a situation that left nothing more to say. She loved to laugh. She minded being laughed *at* as a child minds – in a hurt, silent way – but she loved being teased. Her little vanities were childlike, as were the transparent workings of her mind in simple plots to achieve some desired end; the hints she dropped for something she wanted, which fell with the crash of a brick, were her idea of subtlety. Her faith was like a child's – the sort Christ meant when He said, 'Except ye become as little children' – and her innocence was completely untarnished by her passage through the world. She loved and trusted God utterly, without questioning. In church, murmuring her prayers, she was wrapt, breathless with adoration.

No child that she brought up will ever forget the white-aproned lap and the loving arms and the smell of eau-de-cologne. And one of these will always remember, first among all the cherished memories, how she came through the night-nursery door in answer to the call of a child afraid of the dark, bearing a flaming candle before her, and smiling. She seemed then – and seems still, in memory – like an angel with a flaming sword driving out the powers of darkness and of evil.

THE HERDSMAN

HERE IS a wonderfully enduring quality about field names. Those that are mentioned in deeds 300 years old are still used today whenever an order is given or a day's work discussed, and it is this inclusion in the ordinary, daily life of the farm, rather than the lawyers' writings that has preserved them. Galley Hill, Tilepits, Long Meadow and Beanleaze – the names have passed from one to another through the generations, but the men who spoke them and trod these fields and ploughed their furrow, having gone, become, in less than a century, forgotten. For signs that they passed this way, we can see the walls that they built, the hedges that they planted and laid, but all are anonymous as are the unnamed hummocks in the churchyard where they lie.

Some of us, though, remember back to the days before the tractor, when Mark, the carter, led the huge working horses out of their stables in the morning to harness them to the plough or the waggon or the cart. He was a dour man, and when in a bad mood he would sniff all the time and mutter to himself between his words of encouragement to the horses.

Jim was probably the man whose life on this farm had the longest span of any. He worked here for nearly sixty years, and when he was almost seventy he still worked in the harvest field, forking up the sheaves to the man on the waggon, and keeping pace with his opposite number on the other side to whom he could give forty years or so. In those days, harvest was a team effort, involving everyone on the farm and any spare help available as well, so Jim participated as a matter of course, but that was not his vocation. He was a herdsman, and, if Heaven gives us what has been most beautiful to us in this world, it is hard not to believe that *his* Elysian fields are grazed by a herd of Hereford cattle.

Jim was a good-looking man, with a fine-boned face, hair that had been grey for as long as I could remember, and a light moustache. His eyes were a very clear blue. He was not talkative, and his sparse sentences came out with a jerk as though they were shaken out of him. He had a habit of putting the palm of his hand across his mouth and rubbing the bridge of his nose with the base of his forefinger, and that made it difficult to hear what little he had to say. If something amused him, he would give a small smile (probably, like his words, hidden behind his hand), but I seldom saw him laugh.

He started work on a farm in Oxfordshire at the age of twelve and was paid three shillings a week. His father, also a herdsman, used to wake him daily at 4.30 a.m. He was not, despite these hardships, very keen on the welfare state and used to say that he was better off when he had a very small wage but could buy a pint of beer, an ounce of tobacco and a box of matches for half-a-crown.

Jim's first wife died suddenly and young, leaving him with five children, and after managing uncomfortably for a year or so with the help of his eldest daughter, he took another wife who was kindly and a good cook. When his children had grown up and married, they were apt to visit him, bringing their offspring for him to see, but after a while he would find them a nuisance. Cattle were his life and anything that kept him from them – be it grandchildren or a Bank Holiday – he deplored. One Boxing Day, he was found out in the farmyard in the afternoon and, to an enquiry as to why he had left his fireside, he answered: 'Glad to get a bit o' peace. There's kids crawling all over the place in there and it's Grandad this and Grandad that – I don't know who the 'ell they all are.'

His years on this farm were all spent with the same employer, although to use the words employer and employee in relation to these two men was ridiculous, for they were partners and friends. On the fiftieth anniversary of Jim's coming here, they drank each other's health in whiskey, and when they had both passed their eightieth birthdays they each found the other a convenient excuse.

'I keep the farm on because of old Jim,' the farmer said. 'It would break his heart if he had to retire.'

And Jim would say: 'Course I only goes on because of the boss. Don't want fresh faces about at 'is age.'

Jim did a full day's work until the last year of his life. Then, aged eighty-nine, he consented to shortening his hours a bit. His legs became weak, he took to his bed, and, within two or three weeks, his life began to ebb away.

I saw him on the day he died. He was sleeping a good deal, sometimes conscious, sometimes confused. The parchment-coloured skin was drawn tightly across the bones of his face and hands which were elongated by their thinness, and he looked, as he lay with closed eyes, like a figure in an El Greco picture.

He had always been a God-fearing man, and he knew that at that moment he needed to pray, but his memory would not supply the words. Only, in a low, weak voice, he said over and over: 'Our Father which art in Heaven' and could get no further. But the prayer of Simeon which he had sung at evensong on most Sundays of his life, was answered now. 'Lord, now lettest Thou Thy servant depart in peace.' He died that night.

MUTHU

(O) NE DAY our doorbell rang and a young woman holding a clipboard and a sheaf of papers asked to see the head of the household. When the head – more usually called the Boss – went out to see her, she asked very politely if she could put some questions to him which would not take very long. Puzzled, he asked what sort of questions.

'I am collecting information from which I can produce statistics about the average English household,' she said.

The Boss laughed. 'I'm afraid I can't be much help to you because this is not an average English household. You see, I am Polish, our houseman is Indian and only my wife is English.' She put away her clipboard and went to try another house.

There were very few Indians in England in those days. Muthu had come to us quite by chance. The Boss, who was in the R.A.F., was flying helicopters in Malaya just before we were married and was P.M.C. of the Officers' Mess at Kuala Lumpur. He therefore got to know the staff in the Mess very well, and he wrote to me that several of the boys working there were very keen to come to England. He suggested that perhaps we should bring one of them to help us in our Married Quarter.

'It's a toss-up whether it would work out,' he said, 'but if he's miserable we can just send him home.'

We decided to take the gamble, so then he had to decide which of the applicants would be best for the job. There was one very serious boy who was a Catholic and was very responsible, but, after much thought, he decided on Muthu because he had charm and was always smiling. He did not have the serious attitude to life of the other boy. He rode his bicycle too fast and frequently fell off, causing cuts and bruises. He went to the cinema whenever he could get away, and sometimes when he shouldn't have, and thus spent the money that was meant to pay for his laundry.

He came and told the Boss that he could not get his shirts back as he had spent all his money, and was given a little lecture about not overspending.

'If you're going to be irresponsible like that, I don't know if I can take you to England,' the Boss said.

There was silence and Muthu sniffed and wiped his eye.

'All right. This is to pay for your laundry and if you promise not to do that again you can come to England.'

The Boss, who was coming back on a troop plane, arranged for Muthu to come by ship from Singapore and asked someone he knew to see him on board. But it all seemed rather risky and we were not at all sure that he would be on the ship when it arrived at Southampton. He might have got lost in Singapore or had nerves and decided not to come. But on the appointed day, when the ship came in, the Boss saw Muthu coming down the gangway. That was forty-nine years ago and he has been with us ever since.

Muthu is a Tamil, born In southern India. When he was very small – perhaps one or two – his mother died and his father soon married again. His stepmother did not want him and was unkind to him. He remembers guarding his father's cattle and climbing trees to get coconuts, but his only memory of his mother was that when he was ill with a high fever she wrapped banana leaves round his hot little body to cool him.

After a time, his maternal grandmother felt that he should not be subject any longer to his stepmother's cruelty, so she 'stole' him and took him to live with her. There he was very happy. 'My grandmother very dear lady, very short, no teeth, bring me sweets and give me big hugs.'

His father wanted him back as a work force (aged 6 or 7) but to keep him from the cruel stepmother he was sent to an uncle in Kuala Lumpur who had a little café in which he worked.

The uncle was very strict and beat Muthu if he told a lie. The boy used to pray for his uncle to die; now he feels very guilty about that and says that he is grateful for the discipline his uncle taught him. Only he remembers his sadness when the uncle brought presents for his children but never one for him.

When he got older, the uncle decided it would pay him better if the boy got a job in the R.A.F. Officers' Mess and he would take part of his wages, so that was arranged. Muthu lived in the Mess, his uncle coming for his money every week, and when he went to the cinema be used to see the picture of Piccadilly Circus and he says that he used to, 'pray God my foot one day walk this place.' Nothing, at that time, could have been less likely.

But he came to England, and, as he grew used to the different life, he became, while always loyal to his native India, a keen Anglophile. He learned to cook, taught by a dear friend of ours who was an expert, and he is very proud of the excellent pastry that he makes. He always goes to London for his holidays, thus fulfilling his ambition to tread the stones of Piccadilly Circus, but he avoids August as he says 'there are too many foreigners about then' and he is wary of restaurants because he says he likes 'good English food and no foreign muck'.

When the Boss retired and we exchanged Married Quarters for our own house, we had dogs and he looked after them like babies. The real babies – our son and daughter – he loved, but at first from a distance and then, when they were two or three years old, he adored them, carried them on his shoulders, played 'cricket' with them and was always very gentle and what is called 'a soft touch'. One remembered the stories of the ayahs who looked after the children of the British Raj and saw in him the love of children shown by them.

Muthu loves dogs but is convinced that no other household gives them the loving care that we give ours. Whenever we see a dog waiting outside a shop for its owner or being taken for a walk, he says 'Poor thing'. He insists that our dogs must have the light on all night in the place where they sleep as they would not like the dark.

I tried for a long time, without success, to interest him in birds. When he saw me looking at a film about them on television, he was scornful, but he was converted by the Boss who, after years as a keen and very good shot, had decided that he no longer wanted to kill anything but preferred to watch them. To this end, he put down food for them and Muthu began to help him and – albeit reluctantly – became interested. I started telling him the names of birds seen from the kitchen window but he has his own names for them which would not be recognised by an ornithologist. No matter how often I exhort him to admire the nuthatch stabbing at the bag of nuts outside, he continues to refer to it as 'your friend with big nose.' The jackdaws nesting in the chimneys are to him, quite logically, blackbirds, while the true blackbird, a handsome cock taking worms from the lawn for his family, is 'the one with orange nose.' I have taught him, while driving round the lanes, to salute the magpie and to greet it with 'Your servant, milady' so now he calls that 'the ladybird'. He now, himself, puts out the nuts and sunflower seeds for the birds, and loves to see the great spotted woodpecker come. If, on his walks, he sees a dead bird on the road he tells me, on his return, that he laid it on the grass and asked God to take it to Heaven.

Muthu has happily embraced English superstitions. On his walks across the farm with the dogs, he has collected hundreds of four-leaf clovers and fifteen horseshoes.

When he is going on holiday to London, he always wears a dark suit (of which he has many) and a shirt from Jermyn Street of which he likes to announce the price, remembering long-ago days when he was a little boy who went barefoot and didn't have a shirt. However, in recent years, he has found that this is no longer the 'smart wear' and has felt a bit overdressed among people wearing jeans. So now he wears his dark suit for the train journey and changes into jacket and trousers on arrival at his hotel. The last time he went, I suggested that he would only need to take one bag instead of two if he travelled in his 'smart leisure wear'. He said it would be the same as he would then have to pack his suit. 'But you don't wear it in London,' I said. 'Why take your suit at all?'

He thought for a minute and then shook his head. 'I always take suit. Must do same thing always.'

Muthu is nothing if not a traditionalist.

FINIS.